TOP TEN

S0-AFR-393

GUIDELINES
FOR A GREAT LIFE

Media Ministry
Michiana Fil-Am Church
Berrien Springs, MI 49103

Distributed by Michiana Fil-Am Media Ministry Team
For orders, go to: www.michianafil-am.com/TopTen

Cover by Heidi Magesa
Photography by Wendy Mann
Text Layout & Design by Eric Halder

Printed by Patterson Printing
Benton Harbor, Michigan

Library of Congress
Cataloging-In-Publication Data

Top Ten: Guidelines for a Great Life
  By Ronald A. G. du Preez

  ISBN 0-9786054-2-X

  1. Moral Living – Biblical principles for daily life,
     from the Ten Commandments
  2. Examples and stories illustrating biblical moral
     principles

  du Preez, Ronald A. G.

Additional Books by Ron du Preez: From Omega Media
Post Office Box 407, Berrien Springs, MI 49103, USA
Phone: 1.269.473.3676; Email: faithethics@yahoo.com

Grappling with the Greater Good: Dealing with a Modern Method of Making Moral Decisions

Morals for Mortals: Biblical Roadsigns for Difficult Dilemmas

No Fear for the Future: Affirming Adventism's Divinely-Directed Origin with Ethical Principles for the Endtime People

Pathology of Polygamy: Cross-Cultural Mission on a Biblical Basis

Polygamy in the Bible [Discovering Scriptural Answers on a Vital Controversial Subject]

Putting the "Sabbath" to Rest: A Scriptural Study of Colossians 2:16

Warriors of the Word: Methods of the Messiah for Searching Scripture

Contents

Why This Book?

For several weeks, from January through March 2007, I made a series of presentations on how to live a meaningful life. The response of the listeners showed that the series was appreciated by many, and that it could be a greater blessing if put into print.

At this point, several youth formed a Media Ministry team. Together with others, these youth transcribed all the messages, edited, and proofread; designed a cover; made flyers and advertised the book; set up a secure website; emailed hundreds of potential buyers; negotiated with a printer; and worked feverishly to meet the deadline. A big *Thank You* to all who helped in getting this book into print: Ira Bartolome, Lynda du Preez, Eric Halder, Fares Magesa, Heidi Magesa, Wendy Mann, Dean McDaniel, Rosie McDaniel, Ellie Quinones, Benny Regoso, Beverly Regoso, Arlene Saliba, Aimee Vitangcol, Lope Vitangcol, Jr., and Kevin Wiley.

Also, appreciation is due the Michiana Fil-Am SDA Church for financial and moral support for this project which will doubtless be of great benefit to many. Most vitally, God must be praised for giving us the Ten Commandments – the *Top Ten* – which form the basis for these *Guidelines for a Great Life*.

The New King James Version of the Bible has been the primary translation used in this book. I trust that this study of God's loving expectations will positively impact all who read and implement them.

Ron du Preez, April 2007

Connecting Correctly
Introducing the *Top Ten*

As I was watching a news broadcast of a somber celebration commemorating the life of the fortieth United States president, Ronald Reagan, someone asked, "What is President Reagan's greatest memorial?" The response was quite interesting: "Probably Reagan's greatest memorial is something which is not." At that point the news channel showed flashbacks to Ronald Reagan pointing at the Berlin Wall, and declaring, "Mr. Gorbachev, tear down this wall!" Then the news anchor said, "Today, one billion people are free from Communism as a result of the Reagan legacy."

Liberated to Love

Imagine for a few moments what it must be like to grow up under oppression. Now, I'm not talking about communist oppression. Reflect briefly on a situation of oppression, as described by one who lived under it:

In time, Joseph and each of his brothers died, ending that generation. Then a new king came to the throne of Egypt who knew nothing about Joseph or what he had done. He told his people, "These Israelites are becoming a threat to us because there are so many of them. We must find a way to put an end to this. If we don't, and if war breaks out, they will join our enemies and fight against us. Then they'll escape from the country." So the Egyptians made the Israelites their slaves and put brutal slave drivers over them, hoping to wear them down under heavy burdens.... But the more the Egyptians oppressed them, the more quickly the Israelites multiplied (Exodus 1:6, 8-12 NLT).

The significance of the above statement is found in Deuteronomy 11 – part of Moses' farewell speech, a speech in which Moses is recalling and recapping how God had led the Israelites out of oppression. In verses 2-7 Moses talks about God's miracles, as He brought them out of Egypt – liberated them, and saved them from slavery.

Now we understand why Moses could make a very strong appeal, saying, "Therefore, you shall love the Lord your God, and keep . . . His commandments always" (Deuteronomy 11:1). Because they had been rescued from slavery, they were called upon to respond in loving obedience to the requirements of the God who had redeemed them.

Discovery in Daniel

Recently, I made a "discovery" while reading the Bible. I'd been enjoying my study of the book of Daniel. And here in this ancient record I found something that got me all excited. What do we find Daniel doing during the first year of the reign of Darius, the son of Ahasuerus? He was studying the Bible. Daniel 9:2 notes: "I understood by the books the number of years specified by the word of the LORD, given through Jeremiah the prophet." Verse 3: "Then I set my face toward the LORD God to make requests by prayer and supplications, with fasting, sackcloth, and ashes." So Daniel was praying as well.

Now, let's focus upon verse 4: "And I prayed to the LORD my God, and made confession, and said, 'O LORD, great and awesome God, who keeps covenant and mercy with those who love Him, and with those who keep His commandments.'" As I read this, I said to myself, "That sounds like something I've read before. 'With those who *love* Him, and with those who *keep* His commandments.' I remember a phrase like that in Deuteronomy 7:9."

I had to go back to the original Hebrew language. And you know what? This statement in Daniel 9:2 is a direct quotation from Deuteronomy 7:9. The same words are used. Daniel was actually quoting Deuteronomy 7:9, recalling the phrase about the God who keeps covenant with those who *love* Him and *keep* His commandments.

Love Leads to Loyalty

And that sequence of "love" and "keep" is not unique. Notice that the theme comes up repeatedly, over and over again. We won't take time to look at all of the places in the Old Testament where the "love-and-keep" concept is repeated, but we will look at just a few of them, and only from the book of Deuteronomy. For example, as referred to already above, Deuteronomy 11:1 states: "Therefore, you shall *love* the LORD your God and *keep* His charge." Notice what comes first. "Love" then "keep." By the way, if that is the case, if you *love* the LORD, and therefore you *keep* His law, is there any legalism involved? No, none at all!

God is like a caring parent who doesn't simply say something in only one way. He states it in so many ways. Go to Deuteronomy 11:22 and observe another way that God is trying to get across the same message: "For if you carefully keep all these commandments which I command you today..." My Bible has a long hyphen at this point, and then explains how to "keep" these commandments: "To *love* the LORD your God, to *walk* in all His ways, and to hold fast to Him." So, here it is "love and walk."

Let's look at one more example; this one is found in Deuteronomy 30:20 – "That you may *love* the LORD your God and that you may *obey* His voice, that you may cling to Him." So here's a third phrase: "love and obey." Legalism? Not at all! It's loving loyalty.

Obedience Springs from Honor

Deuteronomy 6:13 states: "You shall *fear* the Lord your God and *serve* Him." Fear? Now wait a minute! When I say the word "fear" in today's context, what does that mean? According to most dictionaries, in today's language "fear" means "afraid." However, when "fear" refers to God, the dictionary explains it with terms such as "awe," "respect," "revere." So in this setting "fear" means to honor God.

By the way, the New Century Version says, "You shall respect the Lord." Today's English Version, the Good News Bible, says, "You shall honor the Lord." The New English Translation says, "Revere the Lord and serve Him."

Deuteronomy 10:12-13 includes more than one concept: "And now, Israel, what does the LORD require of you, but to *fear* the LORD your God, to *walk* in His ways and to *love* Him, to *serve* the LORD your God with all your heart and with all your soul, and to keep the commandments of the LORD and His statutes which I command you today for your good?"

So here we have it again. We had "fear-and-serve," now we've got "fear-and-walk" in His ways; and to love and serve the Lord with all your heart and soul – total loyalty to God.

Loyalists, Not Legalists

Now let me ask you a key question: Do you have any addictions, bad habits, or pet sins? According to Romans 6, we are slaves to the habits and addictions we yield to.

Because we've been redeemed from the oppression of sin, through Jesus Christ's death and resurrection, we can turn to God and say, "Lord, I love you! Thank you for saving me. And because I love You and honor You, I want to serve You, to obey You."

Put simply, to obey God because we love Him demonstrates that we are "loyalists," not legalists.

Divinity's Design for Our Delight

Turn with me to one more verse, which reveals God's wishing only the best for all of us. These words come shortly after the Ten Commandments have been set forth, in the book of Deuteronomy. Notice what God says: "Oh, that they had such a heart in them..." Where does God start? With the heart. If anybody ever accuses you of being a legalist, show that person Deuteronomy 5:29. This is what God says: "Oh, that they had such a heart in them that they would fear Me and always keep all My commandments, that it might be well with them and with their children forever!"

Do you love God? If you love Him, what will be the natural result? Yes, you will choose to keep His commandments, to follow God's *Top Ten*. These are indeed divine *Guidelines for a Great Life*. As Jesus Himself stated so succinctly: "If you love Me, you will keep My commandments" (John 14:15 NASB).

Chapter 1
Smack Back on Track

"And God spoke all these words:
'I, the Lord, am your God,
who brought you from the land of Egypt,
from the house of bondage.
You shall have no other gods before me.'"
(Exodus 20:1-3 NET)

Not too long ago I was in a bookstore looking at various magazines. Since it was towards the end of the year, different magazines seemed to be focused on a similar theme. For example, the cover of *Runner's World* read: "New Year, New You" with the subtitle: "42 Tips to Lose Weight, Get Motivated, Stay Injury Free, and Never Bonk Again" – "bonk" meaning to run out of energy when you are on a long run.

Then, *O Magazine* caught my attention, with a subtitle: "Why It's so Hard to Change Yourself – A Revolutionary Guide to Making it Happen." So, you know what happens when you go into a bookstore. Something catches your eye, you stand, you start reading, and after about five minutes you begin to feel guilty. Conscience whispers, "Hey, if you're going to read this much, you'd better buy it." And I did buy the magazine. And read about dopamine and chemical activities taking place in the brain that affect habits. The article ends with: "You do nothing less than rewire your brain."

That's talking about change, rewiring your brain. The writer says we need to approach change as if we are learning a new language or a new instrument. Obviously we are not going to be fluent in a new language immediately, or to be able to play symphonies after only a couple of lessons. Change demands constant focus and practice.

I visited another bookstore where I spotted a different magazine: *Good Housekeeping*. Again, the cover caught my attention: "Dr. Phil's Four Secrets to Real Change," I began to read, and then bought the magazine as well.

I'd already read about a physical approach to change in *Runner's World*, electro-chemical changes in *O Magazine*, and now the article in *Good Housekeeping* talked about a psychological approach to change. Dr. Phil suggested following four basic steps: (1) identify a specific realistic goal, (2) create a timeline, (3) have a plan of action, and (4) become accountable.

Physical change, electro-chemical change, and psychological change. Among the many possible approaches to change, however, I did not see any magazine dealing with a spiritual approach to change. That's what we want to focus upon here.

Back to the Best Book

Many people make resolutions around the time of the beginning of a new year. As that one magazine proclaimed: "New Year, New You." Yet, too often it seems that these New Year's resolutions don't last beyond January 5 or 6.

How can we do or become radically different or better than the past? You know what I'm talking about, don't you? All of us have failed to achieve our goals or aims during the past. So, there seems to be an innate desire for people to improve, to change, to become better. Yes, but how can we successfully carry out our resolution? How do we get "smack back on track"?

I've talked about three magazine articles that suggested ways to get back on track. I want to suggest, however, a better, indeed the best, "magazine" filled with great "articles" – the Bible. This is it. We need to go back to the Bible.

If I were to ask you to show me in the Bible where to find in the shortest form, the crispest, clearest, simplest guidelines for a great life, where would you direct me?

Exodus 20 – the Ten Commandments!

The Context Is Crucial

Let's consider Exodus 20 with its guidelines for a great life. How does the first commandment begin? Many people start with verse 3: "Thou shalt have no other gods before me." And when I was a child I memorized this great decalogue similarly, beginning with this verse.

However, just as the Jews have rightly recognized, the first commandment actually begins with the previous verse: "I am the LORD your God, who brought you out of the land of Egypt, out of the house of bondage." There it is. That's where it all starts. We'll go on to verse 3 soon, but I want us to clearly recognize that the commandments actually start in verse 2.

Why is it important to start there? If an ancient Israelite heard the words: "I am the LORD your God, who brought you out of the land of Egypt, out of the house of bondage," what would he think of? Yes, redemption, salvation from slavery.

The Lamb Means Life

Go with me to Exodus 12 to consider the actual chronicle of this account. Exodus 12:3 reads: "Speak to all the congregation of Israel, saying: 'On the tenth day of this month every man shall take to himself a lamb, according to the house of his father, a lamb for a household.'"

It starts with a lamb. What were they instructed to do? See verses 6 and 7: "Now you shall keep it until the fourteenth day of the same month. Then the whole assembly of the congregation of Israel shall kill it at twilight. And they shall take some of the blood and put it on the two doorposts and on the lintel of the houses where they eat it." Now, let's read verses 11-13: "And thus you shall eat it: with a belt on your waist, your sandals on your feet, and your staff in your hand. So you shall eat it in haste. It is the Lord's Passover. For I will pass through the land of Egypt on that night, and will strike all the firstborn in the land of Egypt, both man and beast; and against all the gods of Egypt I will execute judgment; I am the LORD. Now the blood shall be a sign for you on the houses where you are. And when I see the blood, I will pass over you; and the plague shall not be on you to destroy you when I strike the land of Egypt." The lamb's blood meant life!

Finally, let's go to verse 51, the last verse of the chapter, where we will see that it is the Passover that was being instituted on that day: "So it came to pass, on that very same day, that the LORD brought the children of Israel out of the land of Egypt according to their armies out of the land of Egypt."

Back to Exodus 20:2. Notice that "memory jogger." God says, "I brought you out of the land of

Egypt!" So, when you read verse 2, your mind goes back to slavery, and from slavery to the sacrificing of the lamb. And most importantly, the lamb points forward to Jesus, as John the Baptizer pointed out: "'Behold! The Lamb of God who takes away the sin of the world!'" (John 1:29). Corroborating that point, the apostle Paul declared in 1 Corinthians 5:7, "For indeed Christ, our Passover, was sacrificed for us." In brief, since the Ten Commandments begin with a definitive reminder of that amazing event of Israel's redemption from Egyptian slavery – through the blood of the lamb – it is very much Christ centered!

Liberty or Licentiousness?

So now we understand why it is correct to recognize that the Ten Commandments begin in Exodus 20:2. We see that the God who redeems has the right to set forth the requirements of a covenant relationship. It is the God who has saved us who now tells us how we should serve Him. If we leave out verse 2, we are in danger, in simple terms, of legalism – just doing something because we *have* to. But verse 2 presents a beautiful picture. We respond to God because He has already redeemed us.

Isaiah 44:22, dealing with spiritual bondage, puts it this way: "I have blotted out, like a thick cloud, your transgressions. And like a cloud, your sins." Now notice the last part of this verse: "Return to Me, for I have redeemed you." God has blotted out our transgressions, our sins, and has invited us wanderers to return to Him as the people He has redeemed.

Just a quick personal illustration: I was born and raised in South Africa, during the time of *apartheid*, i.e., the government's official policy of racial segregation. Even as a child I soon realized that my people were only semi-citizens, since I have a mixed-race heritage. We had the responsibilities of citizenship but not its privileges. I experienced being thrown out of a bus, being beaten by a policeman, and the like because I was raised in a country that oppressed people like me.

The Israelites suffered physical and political oppression. Clearly they were delivered from literal slavery. But, more importantly, this deliverance, this salvation was also spiritual. Slavery to sin is the issue we're considering here. God saved the children of Israel – set them free. And we also have been set free. Think about that for a moment. People say, "Jesus saved me." We are saved by grace through faith. Free at last!

Sadly though, some misinterpret this freedom to mean that they're now free to do whatever they want. From a political perspective, this seems to have happened to many in South Africa when *apartheid* collapsed. Yes, freedom is a wonderful thing, but unfortunately some people throw off all restraint. The new political leaders threw out many things connected with the previous government. Soon abortion became legal. Then the practice of polygamy became legitimate. South Africa was the first country in Africa to make homosexual marriages fully acceptable.

South Africa has become a very dangerous country. Even hundreds of policemen are murdered in one year. South Africa has become the "leader" in the world for people with HIV/AIDS. Unfortunately, it seems that too many have misunderstood being free from oppression to mean freedom to throw morality to the wind.

Ransomed for a Reason

South Africans and all of the rest of us need to spend time in the Word of God and ask, "What does the LORD require of me?" The answer is right there in the Bible. Let's go to Exodus 19:3-4 where Moses recorded God's message to Israel. "And Moses went up to God, and the LORD called to him from the mountain, saying, 'Thus you shall say to the house of Jacob, and tell the children of Israel: "You have seen what I did to the Egyptians, and how I bore you on eagles' wings and brought you to Myself."'" Think about that for a moment. When God saved the Israelites from Egypt, He not only saved them *from* slavery, but He also saved them *to* Himself – from slavery to salvation.

What does this personal God desire? "I am the LORD *your* God." He wants to have a personal relationship with us. He saves us from slavery to sin, and He saves us to Himself. This is the kind of gracious, all-loving God we serve.

If you've been caught speeding and the police officer merely gives you a warning, and then lets you go, how do you respond? Aren't most of us so thankful that we want to jump out of the car and hug the officer?

We're very grateful to a police officer who lets us go without a ticket. How should we feel when we know that we've been saved from slavery to sin? Grateful or not? The first part of the first commandment tells us that we've been set free. The next part of the commandment, that is, verse 3, says that the grateful heart responds to its redemption by having only *one* God, the Redeemer, and none other.

An Assignment for All

Consider the words of Jesus as found in Mark 12. Here Jesus is quoting from Deuteronomy to point out the importance of loving God. When a scribe came and asked Jesus the question, "Which is the first commandment of all?" Jesus responded, "Hear, O Israel the Lord our God, the Lord is one. And you shall love the Lord your God with all your heart, with all your soul, with all your mind, and with all your strength. This is the first commandment" (Mark 12:29-30). I don't know how He could have put it any more plainly. All your heart, emotionally; all your soul, spiritually; all your mind, mentally; all your strength, physically – love God completely.

By this point, there are probably some who have thought, "But I do *not* worship other gods; so this commandment is really not a problem for me!"

So, here's a personal assignment for you to consider. It shouldn't take very long, but it's a vital assignment. It has to do with a biblical concept seen in 2 Corinthians 13:5: "Examine yourselves as to whether you are in the faith. Test yourselves." That's what I'd like you to do. Draw four columns on a sheet of paper. Above Column One put the word "Time." Above Column Two put "Money." Above Column Three place the word "Energy." And above Column Four, "Personal" (which includes anything not in the previous three columns). Track how you generally spend your time during one day; and then do this for an entire week.

Examine how you are using the resources that God has given you. What does this have to do with the first commandment? Although we may not literally be polytheists, serving other gods, we may actually be placing other things ahead of God, and thus be guilty of violating the first commandment. Becoming aware of where we place our priorities, how we use our time, money, energy, etc., may show us where our priorities really are.

Step out of the way and allow, invite, permit God to take the center place in life, the position that He deserves. So let's take inventory, take stock, examine ourselves, see where we are in relationship to God. That is what I consider to be the first guideline for a great life. Let's reprioritize. Make sure we permit God to have first place in our lives; let God take over.

Rules for the Road to Ruin

The importance of prioritizing can be illustrated by my encounter with two professing Christian believers. Both men were having serious spiritual problems. One had slipped back to bad habits he had had before he gave his life to the Lord – dangerous problems with chemical addiction. The other man had behavioral problems. Both were struggling in their walk with the Lord. I visited and prayed with them individually. I asked each a vital question: "How much time do you spend feeding on the Word of God – the Bible?" Their answer – none at all! And yet, they both wanted to have victory over their sinful behaviors.

I asked one of the men, "How much time do you spend watching television? Two hours?"

He said, "No. More."

"Four hours?"

This man, with a full-time job, said, "No."

"How many?"

"Six hours a day."

"Six hours a day?"

"Yeah, I watch from six 'til midnight."

"So you're watching that religious station, 3ABN?"

"No, pastor, not 3ABN."

He was filling his mind with the devil's material, and couldn't figure out why he was having failure in his life!

Providential Protection Provided

It seems so many times that when I read the Bible, I find something new and helpful. That's exciting. For example, I recently reread Genesis 20. I have read this story literally dozens of times. It's about Abraham, who was afraid of being killed because he had a very beautiful wife. Abraham and Sarah connived – lied. Abimelech took Sarah, thinking that she could become his beautiful wife. In verse 5, Abimelech complains to God: "Did he not say to me 'She is my sister'? And, she, even she herself said, 'He's my brother.' In the integrity of my heart and innocence of my hands I have done this." Now, I'd never noticed verse 6 before. "And God said to him in a dream, 'Yes, I know you did this in the integrity of your heart.'" Then God continues: "'For I also withheld you from sinning against me; therefore, I did not let you touch her.'" I said to myself, "Isn't that exciting?" When we make a commitment to God to do His will, sometimes we are made aware of things that we have done innocently. And God will keep us from sinning against Him. Isn't it wonderful? That's the kind of God we serve.

Philippians 2:12-13 corroborates this point; Paul reminds us that God works *in* us to will and to do of

His good pleasure. Also Jude 24 reminds us that God will keep us from falling into sin.

Simple Strategy for Success

Let me ask you a question. How long can a person go without any food or water? A week? I used to say a week. But I've been looking at the 2007 *Guinness Book of World Records*, and learned of a new "record."

On April 1, 1979, Andreas Mihavecz was arrested by the police in Austria, taken to a prison, and put into a holding cell. After putting Andreas into the cell in the jail, the police left him there and forgot all about him. One day went by. Two days went by. Three days went by. One week; two weeks. The police had completely forgotten about Andreas. Two and a half weeks went by and they still did not remember that they had put him in prison. No food, no water! Then suddenly on April 18, 1979, they remembered him. When they opened the door to his cell, they saw that Andreas was close to death. Although not by choice, Andreas Mihavecz had "set" a brand new world record by living without food and water for about eighteen days – almost dying in the process.

What about you? What about me? Spiritually, how long can we survive without the Word of God? We must feed on the Word. Certainly Andreas didn't go without food and water intentionally. And at times circumstances may keep us from reading the Bible. But by choice, let us find time to study the Word. For many of us the best time to spend with the Lord is in the morning before the devil brings all his distractions into our lives.

So, I want to challenge you: Spend time in the Word. Earlier we read Mark 12:30: "You must love the Lord your God with all your heart, all your soul, all your strength, and all your mind." Get your priorities right – allow God to be number one in your life; have no gods besides the true God; commit your life to God; become totally dedicated to the Creator God!

This is the first, and most significant, of the *Guidelines for a Great Life*!

Chapter 2
Search for a Soul Mate

"And God spoke all these words, saying:
*'**You shall not make for yourselves**
a carved image – any likeness of anything*
that is in heaven above, or that is in the
earth beneath, or that is in the water
*under the earth; **you shall not bow down**
to them nor serve them. For I, the Lord*
your God, am a jealous God,
visiting the iniquity of the fathers
upon the children to the third and
fourth generation of those who hate Me,
but showing mercy to thousands,
to those who love Me
and keep My commandments.'"
(Exodus 20:1, 4-6 NKJV)

Some years ago I went to Seoul, South Korea, as a student missionary, but also in search of a soul mate. And, I did find my soul mate there – a fellow student missionary, named Lynda Gill.

When I met Lynda, I was a runner. I discovered that Lynda had been on a gymnastic team. So, we discussed exercising together. I took her resting heart rate. While the average American's resting heart rate was 72, Lynda's was 88 beats per minute.

I said to her, "Lynda, your heart is not strong enough. Let's go jog together." Besides wanting to help Lynda strengthen her physical heart, I was interested in winning her emotional heart as well.

We did go running. In fact, we jogged together regularly for more than a year, never missing a day. Sometimes on a Saturday night we'd be out running at 11:30. We ran faithfully. Can you guess what happened to her heart? Lynda's heart got larger and stronger. Her resting heart rate came down to sixty beats per minute. This progress made us both very pleased. Also, I was happy that she was getting closer and closer to me. In fact, even on our honeymoon we went jogging.

How to Have a Healthy "Heart"

The Bible uses both running and walking as spiritual analogies. Psalm 119:32 states, "I will run in the way of Your commandments, for You shall enlarge my heart." Isn't that interesting?

Now I know there are some who say, "But, I thought that running causes shock to the skeletal system; and that running can cause knee problems."

Right! So, consider 2 John 6: "This is love that we *walk* according to His commandments."

So, if you say, "Hey, I'm too much out of shape for running," then listen to the apostle John and walk. Whatever you do, don't just sit there. Get up and walk or run. For "if you run in God's commandments, it will enlarge your heart."

It is interesting that whether we walk or run, either activity is connected to the issue of love and the heart. So, when we think about the commandments, this is exercise for our spiritual lives. Our hearts will become stronger as we walk and run according to God's law.

From *Who* to *How* to Worship

Let's look now at the second commandment. Exodus 20:4 is the start of a lengthy law: "You shall not make for yourself a carved image, or any likeness of anything that is in heaven above, or that is in the earth beneath, or that is in the water under the earth." Notice the three spheres mentioned here.

By the way, the text does not say that we should not have any sculptures or pictorial representations at all. When we look at the rest of Scripture, we notice that there were beautiful artistic portrayals on the curtains of the Tabernacle. And above the ark of the covenant, there were cherubim representing the angels who are serving the Lord.

Verse 5 continues: "You shall not bow down to them nor serve them." There's the issue – worship!

As I have studied the decalogue, there is one thing that has often confused me. Some people consider Exodus 20:2-6 as one commandment. Others say that verses 2-3 represents one commandment, while verses 4-6 represent another commandment. Which is correct?

Careful scriptural study reveals the following: Verses 2 through 3 form commandment number one, and identifies *who* we should serve; it tells us which God to worship. That's why one must start with verse 2: "I am the LORD your God, who brought you out of the land of Egypt, out of the house of bondage." Our God is Jehovah, the Creator, and the Redeemer.

Commandment number two (verses 4-6) tells us *how* to worship, and how not to worship God. That's the difference. The two commandments are interrelated, very definitively. We cannot separate them. Indeed, the Ten Commandments as a whole are an entire package, with the first commandment directing us to the One worthy of all worship, the One worth all the love of our hearts, minds, and strength, the One who rescued us from the slavery of sin.

The second commandment advises us as to how we should worship our Creator, Benefactor, and Savior.

A Bible story illustrating the difference between the first and second commandments is that of Jehu, as found in 2 Kings 10. Jehu got rid of the worship of Baal – a good thing. But, unfortunately, he still had golden calves – the golden calves set up by Jeroboam. Put simply, Jehu obeyed the first commandment, but failed to keep the second.

Let's look at a statement that captures the essence of this commandment: "The second commandment forbids the worship of the true God by images and similitudes" (*Patriarchs and Prophets*, 306). So that's the issue: worshiping the true God, but in the wrong way.

Beware: We Become What We Behold!

Let's go back to Exodus 20:4: "You shall not make for yourself any carved image." Why is it so important to not worship images?

By divine inspiration, in Deuteronomy 4:15-19, Moses makes a very clear explanation of a vital reason we should avoid idolatry: "Take careful heed to yourselves, for you saw no form when the Lord spoke to you at Horeb [i.e., Mt. Sinai] out of the midst of the fire, lest you act corruptly and make yourselves a carved image in the form of any figure:

the likeness of male or female, the likeness of any animal that is on the earth or the likeness of any winged bird that flies in the air, the likeness of anything that creeps on the ground or the likeness of any fish that is in the water beneath the earth. And take heed lest you lift your eyes to heaven, and when you see the sun, the moon, and the stars, all the hosts of heaven, you feel driven to worship them and serve them, which the Lord your God has given to all the peoples under the whole heaven as a heritage."

In effect God says, "You didn't see any form of Me, so you cannot and must not make an image of Me." As Jesus put it: "God is Spirit, and those who worship Him must worship in spirit and truth" (John 4:24).

Why does it not make sense to worship anything other than God? Psalm 115:4-8 captures it beautifully – almost humorously. Speaking about the Gentiles, it notes: "Their idols are silver and gold, the work of men's hands. They have mouths, but they do not speak; eyes they have, but they do not see; they have ears, but they do not hear; noses they have, but they do not smell; they have hands, but they do not handle; feet they have, but they do not walk; nor do they mutter through their throat. Those who make them are like them; so is everyone who trusts in them."

Let's look at that last verse a bit more carefully. The English Standard Version puts it this way: "Those who make them become like them." The New American Standard Version is even more striking: "Those who make them *will* become like them."

So, instead of worshiping and becoming like these worthless and useless idols, God makes the following summons, seen in Psalm 115:9: "O Israel, trust in the LORD; He is their help and their shield."

Idolatry Is Incredibly Illogical

Let's consider Isaiah 44:6: "Thus says the LORD, the King of Israel, and his Redeemer, the LORD of hosts: 'I am the First and I am the Last; besides Me there is no God.'" Go to verse 8: "'Do not fear, nor be afraid; have I not told you from that time, and declared it? You are My witnesses. Is there a God besides Me? Indeed, there is no other Rock; I know not one.'"

The contrast is very clear. The Bible categorically proclaims that the Creator God is the one true God.

Now let's read the rest of Isaiah 44:9-20, which illustrates the true nature of idolatry: "'Those who make an image, all of them are useless, and their precious things shall not profit; they are their own witnesses; they neither see nor know, that they may be ashamed. Who would form a god or cast a graven image that profits him nothing? Surely all his companions would be ashamed; and the workmen, they are mere men. Let them all be gathered together, let them stand up; yet they shall fear, they shall be ashamed together.

"'The blacksmith with the tongs works one in the coals, fashions it with hammers, and works it with the strength of his arms. Even so, he is hungry, and his strength fails; he drinks no water and is faint.

"'The craftsman stretches out his rule, he marks one out with chalk; he fashions it with a plane, he marks it out with the compass, and makes it like the figure of a man, according to the beauty of a man, that it may remain in the house. He cuts down cedars for himself, and takes the cypress and the oak; he secures it for himself among the trees of the forest. He plants a pine, and the rain nourishes it.

"'Then it shall be for a man to burn, for he will take some of it and warm himself; yes, he kindles it and bakes bread; indeed he makes a god and worships it; he makes it a carved image, and falls down to it. He burns half of it in the fire; with this half he eats meat; he roasts a roast, and is satisfied. He even warms himself and says, "Ah! I am warm, I have seen the fire." And the rest of it he makes into a god, his carved image. He falls down before it and worships it, prays to it and says, "Deliver me, for you are my god."

"'They do not know nor understand.... And no one considers in his heart, nor is there knowledge nor understanding to say, "I have burned half of it in the fire, yes, I have also baked bread on its coals; I have roasted meat and eaten it; and shall I make the rest of it an abomination? Shall I fall down before a block of wood?" He feeds on ashes; a deceived heart has turned him aside; and he cannot deliver his soul, nor say, "Is there not a lie in my right hand?"'"

That's the incredible illogical nature of idolatry! Those who make them will become just like them.

Passion: Punishment and Pardon

Let's go back to Exodus 20:5, for a deeper study. The title for this chapter is: "Search for a Soul Mate." It was the well-known Augustine, I believe, who said, "The soul is restless until it finds its rest in God."

We're all seeking satisfaction. We need somebody to connect with. God is the One who has redeemed us. He wants to have a personal relationship with us.

In the Song of Solomon, the Hebrew term for "jealous" is actually rendered in English as "ardent love." Positively, it is translated as "passion." God is indeed passionate about us.

They say that a mother who loves her children will do anything for them, even die for them. That's the concept here. With passionate love God is "jealous" or zealous for us, because we're formed for that close of a relationship with Him; so He loves us intimately.

But look at the rest of the verse: "A jealous God, visiting the iniquity of the fathers upon the children to the third and fourth generations of those who hate me."

Wait a minute! You're kidding! So, the children are going to pay for their father's sins? Hold on!

Deuteronomy 24:16 helps put these words into perspective: "The fathers shall not be put to death for their children, nor shall the children be put to death for their fathers; a person shall be put to death for his own sin."

One commentator has written: "It is inevitable that children should suffer from the consequences of parental wrongdoing, but they are not punished for the parents' guilt, except as they participate in their sins. It is usually the case, however, that children walk in the steps of their parents. By inheritance and example the sons become partakers of the father's sin. Wrong tendencies, perverted appetites, and debased morals, as well as physical disease and degeneracy, are transmitted as a legacy from father to son, to the third and fourth generation. This fearful truth should have a solemn power to restrain men from following a course of sin" (*Patriarchs and Prophets*, 306).

Now, consider the positive effect on those who choose correctly: "But showing mercy to thousands, to those who love Me and keep My commandments" (Exodus 20:6). The New Revised Standard Version puts it this way: "But showing steadfast love to the thousandth generation of those who love me and keep my commandments." In the broader context, that's what it should be–"Thousandth generation," as is seen in Deuteronomy 7:9: "Therefore know that the LORD your God, He is God, the faithful God who keeps covenant and mercy for a thousand generations with those who love Him and keep His commandments." Exodus 20:6 is virtually echoed in Deuteronomy. Yes, God brings judgment to those who reject Him. But God is a merciful God, to those who love and obey.

In fact, one commentator noted that the third-and-fourth generation reference relates to evildoers, while thousandth generations relates to good – four versus a thousand. Yes, God is all merciful!

Idolatry Is an "Inside" Issue

Now here's my question: Have you ever visited a home where somebody actually worships images? Yes, we may have friends who are part of some religious persuasions which make use of idols. But generally, when we think about carved images and people worshiping them, we think of Buddhism or Hinduism in Asia or animism in Africa.

Therefore, some may claim: "But, I don't worship idols or images. I don't have that problem."

Go now to Ezekiel 14:2-3. Remember, the issue is not *whom* we should worship, but *how*. "And the word of the LORD came to me, saying, 'Son of man, these men have set up their idols in their *hearts*.'" Wow! Now we have no way that we can say, "I don't worship idols." Here it is. What does the Bible say? "These men have set up idols in their hearts."

John Calvin, the great Protestant Reformer, put it this way: "The human heart is a perpetual factory of idols." A perpetual factory of idols! The book, *The Great Controversy* reads: "It is as easy to make an idol of false doctrines and theories as to fashion an idol of wood or stone. By misrepresenting the attributes of God, Satan leads men to conceive of Him in a false character. With many, a philosophical idol is enthroned in the place of Jehovah; while the Living God, as He is revealed in His word, in Christ, and in the works of creation, is worshiped by but few" (page 583).

The same author queried: "Are we worshipers of Jehovah, or of Baal? of the living God, or of idols? No outward shrines may be visible; there may be no image for the eye to rest upon; yet we may be practicing idolatry. It is as easy to make an idol of cherished ideas or objects as to fashion gods of wood or stone. Thousands have a false conception of God and His attributes. They are verily serving a false god as were the servants of Baal" (*Review and Herald*, March 12, 1908).

Wow! We may have philosophical idols. We have idols in the heart, while "few" are worshiping the true God – the Creator God of the Bible.

In a nutshell, idolatry is an internal issue. It all begins on the inside.

Which idols are you and I guilty of worshiping?

Where's the "Word" in Our Worship?

Someone once commented: "We make an idol whenever we worship an image rather than listening to the Word."

One of the problems with physical images of God is that they distract us, thus keeping us from hearing the Word. On Mt. Sinai, God revealed Himself through audible words. He did not want the people to look at Him. Rather, He wanted the people to listen to what He had to say. The above-quoted writer says: "The image wants to distract us from hearing the Word." He identifies some of those images: "The crucifix, the icon, the drama, and the dance. These things are not aids to worship, but make true worship all but impossible."

Whoa! Such strong words: These things distract us, and "make true worship all but impossible."

Reading Ezekiel 22:26 shook me awake: "Her priests have violated My law and profaned My holy things; they have not distinguished between the holy and unholy, nor have they made known the difference between the unclean and the clean; and they have hidden their eyes from my Sabbaths, so that I am profaned among them."

And, of course, we remember the words of Jesus in Matthew 15:9: "In vain do they worship me, teaching as doctrines the commandments of men." So when we come to the issue of corporate worship, this is what I want to challenge all of us to do. I would like, by God's grace, for all of us to ask ourselves seriously: When we go for corporate worship, are we focusing upon how we can worship God without any of these distractions? Many times, without meaning to, we become distracted. For example, we can be distracted from true worship by how music sounds or is performed.

Time magazine, in its November 6, 2006 edition, had an interesting article entitled, "In Touch With Jesus." In part, it stated: "Youth ministers have been on a long and frustrating quest of their own over the past two decades or so, believing that a message wrapped in pop-culture packaging was a way to attract teens to their flocks. Pastors watered down the religious content and boosted the entertainment. But in recent years churches have begun offering their young people a style of religious instruction grounded in Bible study and teachings about the doctrines of their denomination. Their [i.e., the pastors'] conversion has been sparked by the recognition that sugar-coated Christianity popular in the 1980s and the 1990s has caused a growing numbers of kids to turn away, not just from attending youth fellowship activities, but also from practicing their faith at all."

Interesting! Pastors and youth leaders are waking up to the fact that their attempts to attract the youth by means of "idolatrous" methods of the world have actually driven youth away.

What is that a call for us to do? Yes, to get serious.

We know *whom* we should worship. So let's get serious about *how* we should worship the true God.

The Accused and the Apparel

At times when I've watched news coverage of someone being arrested, I see an unshaven person wearing grungy, sloppy jeans. Then later in the news broadcast I see the same person in orange prison garb. But when the accused comes before the judge and jury for trial, I hardly recognize the person, now dressed in a business suit, clean shaven, hair nicely combed – looking like a refined gentleman.

Where is the accused? Where is the criminal? When he comes to stand before the judge, the accused wants to look his best. He wants the jury and the judge to see him as a fine, upstanding citizen.

When we come to church, we come not simply as accused criminals, but as guilty sinners. Thus, we come guilty before the Great Judge of the universe. One wonders: Should we not similarly dress our best, to appear in such a way that we demonstrate that we are serious about coming before the King, that we respect the Judge of the entire universe? Let's get serious! Let's think about the best ways for us to worship God.

Now, I'm not about to specify what you should wear. But I am talking about modesty, simplicity – principles of Scripture that are all there. How should we appear before God?

Obviously people of various cultures dress in ways fitting for those cultures. People of good taste wear neat and modest clothing in keeping with the culture – not attracting attention to self but directing attention to Jesus Christ. For the North American cultural setting, Amy Vanderbilt says that what we wear for any occasion should be "unremarkable."

Putting People in Perilous Places

An idol can be anything or anyone that we try to put in place of God or that dulls another person's sensitivity to the presence of God. Who are the people who may become idols or icons? Are they the kinds of people seen on the TV program "American Idol"?

Who is it that we look up to? Admiring other people can be dangerous. Recently, I listened to a preacher share a message that brought us closer to God. When the message was over, a couple of Christian commentators, instead of talking about the message, talked about the preacher. He had preached his heart out about the dangers of idolatry. But when he was finished, all the commentators talked about was what an incredible preacher he was. They never talked once about the message he had shared.

They missed the message against idolatry, and turned him into an idol – the irony of it. And we all face the same danger. I praise God for teachers – teachers who lead people to the Lord, teachers who help students learn. But sometimes students begin to idolize the teacher. And some parents say, "Oh, that's the greatest teacher that my kids have ever had!" Rather, how about saying: "That teacher brought our children to the Lord. Praise the Lord!" Don't praise the teacher. Don't praise the pastor. Praise the Lord. We must not idolize the people who help us to come close to God. That is dangerous not only for us but also for the one idolized.

The Solution? The Savior!

We can turn anything or anyone into an idol. God is challenging us to shun all forms of idolatry; to do what pleases God, to keep God first in everything. What a wonderful privilege to have been made in the image of God. Let's not spoil that image by creating artificial ones that compete with our worship of God.

Let us focus our admiration upon Jesus – the One "who being the brightness of His glory and the express image of His person, and upholding all things by the word of His power, when He had by Himself purged our sins, sat down at the right hand of the Majesty on high" (Hebrews 1:3), the One who merits all of our adoration and praise.

Let us abide in Christ. In John 15:4, Jesus reminds us: "'Abide in Me, and I in you. As the branch cannot bear fruit of itself, unless it abides in the vine, neither can you, unless you abide in Me."

Our only hope of living a victorious life free from idolatry is for us to abide in Christ. Only by abiding in Christ can we properly reflect the image of God that He wants people to see through us, both within the community and within the church.

Chapter 3
Come Out of the "Closet"

"And God spoke all these words:
'You shall not take the name
of the LORD your God in vain,
for the LORD will not hold guiltless
whoever takes his name in vain.'"
(Exodus 20:1, 7 NET)

In 1984 I began to consciously collect the various ways in which people have misspelled my last name. My family name is "du Preez," a name originating in France, but not very well-known outside South Africa. Looking at the lighter side of the way my name has been misspelled, I decided to put together a collection of these goofs in a book labeled: "Look at What They've Done to My Name." By 1997 I had recorded more than 200 ways in which my last name had been misspelled.

Here are a few examples: Some have made the name into a Hispanic sounding one, "Ron du *Perez*." While flying on a plane, I received a vegetarian meal with "Durtreez" attached to the container. Now you should see what they've done to my wife Lynda's name. People have called her "Lynda *lu* Preez," "Lynda *bu* Preez," "Lynda *ju Frez*," and "Lynda du *Freez*." My name has been abbreviated as "Dr. Ronald du." But then, others have lengthened it to "Ronald du Preez du Preez." In brief, people have really slaughtered my name.

Why are names so important?

I've had the opportunity to teach at the Amazing Facts Center of Evangelism. Before going to California, I've asked those in charge to send me pictures of all their students. I've studied those pictures carefully, trying to memorize what name goes with which face. Then, when I get there, I can walk in and say, "Hi Gary. How are you?" Of course, surprised, Gary responds, "How do you know me?" Students ask: "How come you know us, except for one or two of the women who've changed their hairstyles?" Then, I tell them my "secret"– how I have been learning their names by studying their pictures. And the students *really* appreciate it– for people like to be called by their names.

Understandably, when we become too busy we sometimes forget people's names. But I've found out that remembering names is important. If you meet somebody years later and can say, "Hey John, how are you doing?" John brightens up; his smile goes from ear to ear. "You remembered my name!"

We all have names, some of them difficult to pronounce or to remember, but if we want to show respect to others, we learn their names – pronounce them correctly and remember them. Yes, names are very important.

The Meaning of the Mandate

Go with me now to a study of the third commandment – a commandment dealing with the *name* of God. Why did God give us the third commandment as a guideline for a great life? We need to take some time to reflect on that, to think about it. What does this commandment mean for us in our daily lives?

So let's go to the Bible – Exodus 20:7: "You shall not take the name of the LORD, your God, in vain. For the LORD will not hold him guiltless who takes his name in vain." The word in the Hebrew language for "in vain" is an expression that means "falsehood," "vanity," "emptiness," "nothingness," "uselessness."

Notice how various translations put it. For example, a Jewish translation called Tanakh renders it: "You shall not swear falsely by the name of the LORD, your God, for the LORD will not clear one who swears falsely by His name." Now you can take this to the legal setting in court where you are asked to swear on the Bible that you will "tell the truth and nothing but the truth, so help me, God."

1. Blasphemy

Let's go to a biblical concept found in Leviticus 24. This is the first misuse of God's name that we want to look at. How is God's name misused? This chapter tells a fascinating but very sad story of two men who have gotten into an altercation. It wasn't just a matter of words. Notice verse 10: "Now the son of an Israelite woman, whose father was an Egyptian, went out among the children of Israel; and this Israelite woman's son and a man of Israel fought each other in the camp." They were fighting. A real brawl. Verses 11-14: "And the Israelite woman's son blasphemed the name of the LORD and cursed; and so they brought him to Moses. (His mother's name was Shelomith, the daughter of Dibri, of the tribe of Dan.) Then they put him in custody, that the mind of the LORD might be shown to them. And the LORD spoke to Moses saying, 'Take outside the camp him who has cursed; then let all who heard him lay hands on his head, and let all the congregation stone him.'" To verse 16 now: "And whoever blasphemes the name of the LORD shall surely be put to death." Very serious, folks.

Put simply, blasphemy is the first example, seen in Leviticus 24, of how the name of the LORD can be taken in vain, used as a curse – a direct attack on God, cursing God's name, misusing God's name.

2. Profanity

When Jesus taught the disciples to pray, He said, "In this manner, therefore, pray: 'Our Father in heaven, hallowed be Your name'" (Matthew 6:9). God's name is to be hallowed – to be held sacred.

Why? Think about this for a moment. What do parents do who are expecting or adopting a child? Do they merely put hundreds of names into a hat, then draw out a name at random? Hardly! Why not? Because names have meaning. They are tied in with our identity. They have to do with our character.

Similarly, God's name is directly connected to His very identity, His very essence. In Exodus 33:19 Moses records God's words: "Then he said, 'I will make all My goodness pass before you, and I will proclaim the name of the LORD before you.'" What does "I will proclaim the name" mean? What is the proclamation? Notice what immediately follows in the biblical text: "I will be gracious to whom I will be gracious, and I will have compassion on whom I will have compassion." When God says "I will proclaim my Name," He then declares what *kind* of a God He is. He declares His character: "I will be compassionate. I will be gracious."

We know that the personal name of God, Yahweh or Jehovah, indicates that He is the Omniscient, the Omnipresent, the Omnipotent God.

For example, Psalm 99:3 indicates that the name of God is intimately connected with His character: "Let them praise your great and awesome name – He is holy." God's name and character are intimately connected. His name is holy.

The same idea re-echoes in Psalm 111:9: "Holy and awesome is His name." Again, the idea is clear. God's name is holy, so it must be treated that way. The Darby Bible, translated in the 1800's, says: "Thou shalt not idly utter the name of Jehovah thy God, for Jehovah will not hold him guiltless that idly uttereth His name" (Exodus 20:7). This is often what we think of when talking about not taking the Lord's name in vain – that is, not idly using God's name.

A more obvious way of violating God's name involves using it as an expression of surprise – "O My God!" These three words are used so commonly that you'll see them in print as one word– "omigod!" And even professing Christians use this term, perhaps unaware that they are actually taking God's name in vain. The English dictionary notes that there are several other phrases used, such as "gosh," "gee," etc., which are all actually different ways in which the name of God or Jesus is used as expletives, as a form of profanity.

In addition, because we are made in the image of God and must respect God's name, we must also respect our bodies. Unfortunately, it's common nowadays for people to flippantly refer to parts of the human body – especially the private parts. All of these terms have now become part of profanity. Take note of Ephesians 5:1-4: "Be imitators of God. Walk in love.... But fornication and all uncleanness or covetousness, let it not even be named among you, as is fitting for saints; neither filthiness nor foolish talking, nor coarse jesting, which are not fitting, but rather giving thanks." So, very clearly, we are called upon to keep away from any profanity– a very common way of taking God's name in vain.

3. Mercenary

Let's consider now a third way in which people sometimes misuse God's name. The New International Version reads: "You shall not misuse the name of the Lord your God, for the Lord will not hold anyone guiltless who misuses His name" (Exodus 20:7). I call this mercenary because as I listen, as I watch, I find many people claiming the name of God for monetary purposes. What do I mean?

Let me illustrate. Remember Evel Knievel? Some decades ago, Evel Knievel was a well-recognized dare-devil who used to do all kinds of stunts, mainly on motorcycles. In 1974 he tried to jump a motorcycle across the Snake River canyon. Many remember that spectacular failure when his rocket-powered motorcycle eventually went down into the canyon. He survived somehow.

But listen to this. In 2001 Evel Knievel (whose real name is Robert Craig Knievel) registered his name as a trademark. Since that time he has sold toys and merchandise bearing his name and his likeness which have brought in almost a third of a billion dollars. Remember how he used to dress in that white suit and a v-neck? Notice what happened recently. Rap artist Kanye West put out a video called "Touch the Sky," which cost him a million dollars to produce. Kanye West dressed like Evel Knievel and, with computer technology, also went across the canyon and "touched the sky." Reportedly the video is filled with immorality and profanity.

You probably can guess what happened next. The real Knievel filed a lawsuit in federal court in Tampa, Florida claiming infringement on his trademark *name* and likeness. Knievel says, "The guy Kanye West just went too far using me to promote his filth to the world; using my *name* to make money." Knievel says, "I'm not in any way that kind of a person."

Mercenary use of another's name. Recently, I heard an interviewer ask a very popular contemporary pop singer: "How is it that you have been such a success?" Guess what this singer, whose songs apparently were number one for several weeks, said. "Oh, I want to thank God." And I thought, "Thank God?" And then she went further: "And I want to thank Jesus Christ for my success." I asked myself, "Is she a Christian?" But then I reflected on the kind of music she sang, the lyrics, and the kind of dancing she did; and, I said to myself, "This is using God's name in vain – for a monetary purpose. Because those who listen will say, 'Ah, she says she's a Christian; therefore, this must be good music.' And then, they'll buy her CD's."

Be careful of what we might call imposters – not only musicians, but also some sports stars, and even politicians, especially when it gets close to election time. Now, some may be genuine, but you know what I'm saying. There are some who do not live as Christians at all, but they use this strategy to get votes, so they can be back in power. That is another way to take God's name in vain. Incidentally, there's a fascinating story in the Bible, found in Acts 19, which illustrates the dangers of the mercenary misuse of God's name.

4. Hypocrisy

There is a fourth way in which God's name can be taken in vain. Consider this time the New Revised Standard Version: "You shall not make wrong use of the name of the Lord your God, for the Lord will not acquit anyone who misuses His name" (Exodus 20:7). Think about this for a moment. When one is baptized, that person takes the name of Jesus and is called a Christian. Quoting Matthew 28:19 at the baptism, a pastor says: "I now baptize you 'in the name of the Father, and the Son, and the Holy Spirit.'" In the Name! When we become Christians, we take on the name of Jesus. We are baptized in the Name.

Incidentally, that's why I've titled this chapter "Come Out of the Closet!" In the old King James Version, the Bible says that a Christian should "enter into thy closet" to pray. If, as a Christian, you are spending time praying, you're developing a personal relationship with Jesus Christ. The challenge to us is to then "come out of the closet," that is, to step out, to live as Christians under the name of Jesus Christ. To be *real* Christians, both at home as well as outside the home.

Allow me to illustrate. Imagine that you have just received a major promotion, and want to go and celebrate at your favorite restaurant – with Mexican food. You are new in the town, and find directions to Don Pablos Mexican restaurant. You walk in and order some delicious enchiladas, only to hear the waiter respond, "Sorry, we don't have any enchiladas; but we do have wonderful seafood."

"Seafood! You're kidding. Well, can I have some tacos?"

"Sorry, we don't have any tacos either. But, we've got some great fried fish! You'd love 'em. We have a guy direct from Japan. He was the best chef in Tokyo. He's now come to the USA. Here he is." And the guy gently bows in greeting. He doesn't even speak English.

"Look, all I want is some good Mexican food – don't you have some bean burritos?"

"No! But we've got really good teriyaki."

By this time, you realize there's a problem somewhere. So, you ask: "Is this not called Don Pablos Mexican restaurant?"

"Yes, it is! But, we actually do not sell any Mexican food; only Japanese!"

Firmly, yet kindly, you will likely reply, "You folk are imposters!" And you'll walk out of there, feeling that you've wasted your time.

Sadly, like that Japanese restaurant masquerading as a Mexican restaurant, Christians can sometimes also be guilty of hypocrisy – when we take the name "Christian," but really act like and live like the rest of society. Does the name we bear on the "outside" reflect what is on the inside? Hypocrisy is perhaps the most subtle and most dangerous way of taking God's name in vain. We must not wrongfully use God's name by claiming to be Christians while living a worldly life.

The Call to Commitment

As we have seen, there are various ways that we can take God's name in vain. The challenge is for us to live as Christians – to live out Jesus' life in us.

Let me share with you a statement that beautifully summarizes what we have been saying:

"This commandment not only prohibits false oaths and common swearing, but it forbids us to use the name of God in a light or a careless manner, without regard to its awful significance. By the thoughtless mention of God in common conversation, by appeals to Him in trivial matters, and by the frequent and thoughtless repetition of His name, we dishonor Him. 'Holy and reverent is His name' (Psalm 111.9). All should meditate upon His majesty" (*Patriarchs and Prophets*, 306-307).

That's the key. Rather than thinking, "Oh, I shouldn't say these things," focus upon God and His majesty. And the more time we spend with God, the more time we spend with Jehovah in His Word, the less likely we will be to take His name in vain in any of the ways we've talked about.

Let's finish the paragraph I started sharing above: "All should meditate upon His majesty, His purity, and holiness, that the heart may be impressed with a sense of His exalted character; and His holy name should be uttered with reverence and solemnity."

The lawsuit I mentioned above, initiated by Robert Craig Knievel against Kanye West, has interesting implications. Knievel sued West to pay for damages done to the Knievel name. And "the Lord will not hold guiltless" those who take His name in vain, whether it be through blasphemy, profanity, being a mercenary, or through hypocrisy.

1 Corinthians 6:11 brings us good news. Although we may have been ensnared in various kinds of evil, including taking the Lord's name in vain, we can claim Paul's words: "But you were washed, but you were sanctified, but you were justified in the name of the Lord Jesus and by the Spirit of our God."

Let us bring honor to the name of God by letting His Spirit live in us each day. Let's "come out of the closet," and rightly live as Christians, to reflect the glory of God's holy name.

Chapter 4
The "Rest" of the Story

"And God spoke all these words, saying:
'Remember the Sabbath day,
to keep it holy. Six days you shall labor
and do all your work, but the seventh day
is the Sabbath of the LORD your God.
In it you shall do no work:
you, nor your son, nor your daughter,
nor your male servant, nor your female
servant, nor your cattle, nor your stranger
who is within your gates. For in six days
the LORD made the heavens and the earth,
the sea, and all that is in them,
and rested the seventh day.
Therefore the LORD blessed
the Sabbath day and hallowed it.'"
(Exodus 20:1, 8-11 NKJV)

We've been considering "guidelines for a great life." Psalm 119:32 talks about running as part of that good life: "I will run in the way of Your commandments, for You shall enlarge my heart." Of course, physically, running gives us good exercise and that enlarges our hearts. For those who love walking, 2 John 6 uses walking as a beautiful analogy: "This is love, that we walk according to His commandments."

For many years serious, runners have tried to run every single day, without ever taking time off. Some have actually run daily for twenty or twenty-five years straight! Some competitive walkers have tried the same – these folk, who never take a day off, are called "streakers."

The fortieth-year special edition of *Runner's World* carries an article making a suggestion to such "streakers." Advice from the best runners in the last several decades is as follows: "Every week take one day off from running. That day off gives you a definite beginning and end to your training week and encourages the body to recover.... A weekly break also keeps you mentally fresh." So much for the fifteen, twenty, or twenty-five years of streaking, without missing a day. They are wrong! The best advice? Make sure you take off one day per week.

What does that sound like? Yes, like a weekly rest day that God set aside – the Sabbath!

The Seventh Day Sanctified

So, let's go all the way back to the very beginning, to Genesis 2. I need to go there because some people say, "Oh, the Ten Commandments. You only get them in Exodus 20. They were given to the Israelites specifically on Mt. Sinai. They are not for all people."

In fact, a book by a well-known, well-respected Lutheran Old Testament scholar, Dr. Walter Kaiser, titled *Toward Old Testament Ethics*, aptly points out: "It must not be thought that the Decalogue was inaugurated and promulgated at Sinai for the first time" (page 82). Interesting! Dr. Kaiser goes on to note: "All Ten Commandments had been part of the law of God, previously written on the heart instead of on stone, for all ten appear, in one way or another, in Genesis" – ingrained within the heart, instead of in granite.

Dr. Kaiser gives examples, such as Cain's breaking the sixth commandment when he killed Abel; Joseph's being tempted by Potiphar's wife to break the seventh commandment, but responding: "How can I do such a great wickedness and sin against God?" (Genesis 39:9). Then Dr. Kaiser points us to Genesis 2 as a reference to the fourth commandment.

So, let's spend a few minutes in Genesis 2. The context is the creation story: "Thus the heavens and the earth, and all the host of them, were finished. And on the seventh day God ended His work which He had done, and He rested on the seventh day from all His work which He had done." Verse 3: "Then God blessed the seventh day and sanctified it, because in it He rested from all His work which God had created and made." God rested from His work.

Now, here's my question: of the animals, of the plants, of human beings, who alone are made in the image of God? Human beings. Right! Inasmuch as we are made in God's image, we can be expected to follow His example. God rested. We rest. God took time, rested from His work. We are to take time, to rest from all our work.

God blessed the Sabbath – sanctified it, meaning that the day was set apart for a holy purpose. And God did this right at the beginning of time on earth– at the end of creation week.

Let me ask a question: How do we know what a year is? Where do we get that idea? It's based on the time that it takes for the earth to rotate around the sun. How about a month? Where do we get that idea? Month sounds like the word "moon." The month is basically measured by the cycle of the moon as it rotates around the earth. How about a day? From the earth's complete rotation on its axis.

Now to the final question: Astronomically, where do we get the idea of the week? There is no astronomical data or information showing us the length of a week. Where's the only place from which we get the week? The Bible, right! Dr. Walter Kaiser is correct in saying that the weekly cycle goes back to Genesis. We don't start in Exodus with the Ten Commandments. We go right back to Genesis.

Seven-Day Cycle Before Sinai

In various places in the Book of Genesis there are hints of a seven-day cycle. Here are a few examples. Genesis 7:4: "For after seven more days I will cause it to rain." Now go to verse 10: "And it came to pass after seven days...." Go with me to Genesis 8:10: "And he waited yet another seven days...." Now verse 12: "So he waited yet another seven days." We find this kind of a seven-day cycle repeated right here in the book of Genesis, showing that a basic weekly cycle was a well-known phenomenon even before we get to the book of Exodus.

Go with me now to Exodus 5. Remember that the Israelites were slaves in Egypt. They suffered under oppression. Exodus 5:1-2 notes: "Afterward, Moses and Aaron went in and told Pharaoh, 'Thus says the LORD God of Israel: Let My people go, that they may hold a feast to Me in the wilderness.' And Pharaoh said 'Who is the LORD, that I should obey His voice to let Israel go? I do not know the LORD, nor will I let Israel go.'" Go with me now to verse 5.

Something has happened between verses 3 and 4. Verse 5: "And Pharaoh said, 'Look, the people of the land are many now, and you make them *rest* from their labor.'" Interesting!

From what roots in Hebrew does the word "rest" come? Yes, from *shabbath*. A Seminary professor friend shared something I had not noticed before. In modern language, Pharaoh said to Moses and Aaron: "You make them sabbatize. You make them rest from their labors." Fascinating!

Notice how the book *Patriarchs and Prophets* puts it: "He [i.e., Pharaoh] added, 'Behold the people of the land are now many and ye make them rest from their burdens.' In their bondage, the Israelites had to some extent lost the knowledge of God's law. The Sabbath had been generally disregarded. The efforts made [by Moses and Aaron] to restore the observance of the Sabbath had come to the notice of their oppressor" (pages 257-258).

There it is. Moses and Aaron had tried to bring the people back to keeping God's law, including the fourth commandment, which was later reiterated in spoken and written form on Mt. Sinai, as recorded in Exodus 20.

The Day – A Divine Delight

But at this point in the story the Israelites had not had the Mt. Sinai experience. Look at Exodus 16:23: "Then he [i.e., Moses] said to them, 'This is what the LORD has said: "Tomorrow is a Sabbath rest, a holy Sabbath to the LORD. Bake what you will bake today, and boil what you will boil; and lay up for yourselves all that remains, to be kept until morning."'"

Come with me on a short tangent to Isaiah 58:13-14. I want to add in a little bit here. Isaiah 58 talks about what God expects of people – how we should live as serious, committed believers: "If you turn away your foot from the Sabbath, from doing your pleasure on My holy day, and call the Sabbath a delight, the holy day of the LORD honorable, and shall honor Him, not doing your own ways, nor finding your own pleasure, nor speaking your own words, then you shall delight yourself in the LORD; and I will cause you to ride on the high hills of the earth, and feed you with the heritage of Jacob your father. The mouth of the LORD has spoken."

"Turn away your foot," means don't desecrate. Isaiah defines Sabbath rest as "not doing your own ways, nor finding your own pleasure, nor speaking your own words, then you shall delight." If we take delight in the Lord's delight, we will find delight: "You shall delight yourself in the LORD; and I will cause you to ride on the high hills of the earth, and feed you with the heritage of Jacob your father. The mouth of the Lord has spoken." There it is! The Sabbath is a delight. We should enjoy it.

That seminary professor who pointed us to the Sabbath implied in Exodus 5:5, makes sure that every Sabbath is a delight – from Friday evening when the sun sets until Sabbath evening when the sun sets. Especially when they had children at home, she and her husband made special plans to celebrate the Sabbath as a blessed, delightful day so that when Saturday night came, the children would say, "Oh no! The Sabbath is going to be over. We have to wait six more days before we can again enjoy this special day with God."

Many of us fail to "remember" the Sabbath in this manner – to carefully plan for it. I remember with chagrin when I was a student at Andrews University, and our nephews Danny and Patrick were living with us. One week I had worked so long and hard that when Sabbath came, the only thing I wanted to do was rest – sometimes referred to as "lay activities," badly misinterpreted. The boys were somewhere between five and nine. Yet we wanted to make the Sabbath a delight for them. So what did we do? We played Bible charades.

And I'll admit that my mind raced at full speed thinking of every Bible character I could play who would be lying down. I was Goliath after he had been slain, so I could lie on the floor until the kids guessed what part I was playing. Another time when my turn came, I believe I was Jonah in the belly of the great fish – lying on my belly this time. Next time I may have played the part of Lazarus before he was called from the dead. Every time, I looked for some way I could lie down. The kids loved it, though they never knew why I was acting out the parts of Bible characters who were lying down. Yes, I had *not* remembered the Sabbath during the week, so as to be able to really enjoy the day as God intended it.

Let's return briefly to Exodus 16:25, which talks about preparing for the Sabbath, preparing so that we won't desecrate God's holy day – the seventh-day Sabbath. Talking about the manna collected the day before, Moses said, "Eat that today, for today is a Sabbath to the LORD; today you will not find it in the field. Six days you shall gather it, but on the seventh day, which is the Sabbath, there will be none." Now look at verse 27: "Now it happened that some of the people went out on the seventh day to gather, but they found none."

There are always some of us who really don't believe what God says. We say, "Now I'm going to go check, just to see." Verse 28 states: "And the Lord said to Moses, 'How long do you refuse to keep my commandments and my laws?'"

But verse 30 notes: "So the people rested on the seventh day."

"Remember" Is Not Merely Mental

Turn now to Exodus 20. We've been studying through the Ten Commandments. This is clearly a most important commandment. Why do I say "most important?" In the Hebrew language, this commandment is at least five words longer than any of the other commandments. If we were to divide up the Ten Commandments by word count into three sections, we would have the first three commandments as the first set of about sixty-something words in Hebrew; then we'd have the fourth commandment as the second set with sixty-something words; and finally we'd have the last six commandments as the third set with sixty-something words. So the middle set of words turns out to be the heart of the Ten Commandments.

This commandment begins with what word? "Remember" – a Hebrew infinitive not limited to time. The commandment calls us to "remember," not only by looking back to creation but also by looking forward.

Let's imagine that you are married and that your wedding anniversary has arrived. That morning your spouse turns to you and says, "Honey, do you know what today is?"

And you say, "Oh yeah, I know. I've been thinking about it. I've remembered for the last week. I've been thinking about it, and I remembered."

Not sure that you really remember, your spouse asks: "So, what day is today?"

"It's our anniversary! I told you I remembered it!"

"What do you mean you remembered it? What plans have you made? What are we going to do today?"

"Oh nothing, but I remembered it."

How many spouses would be happy with someone who "remembers" the anniversary in that "spectacular" way? Not many.

When God says to remember this important anniversary of the creation of this world, it's not simply a mental thing: "Oh yes, God, I remembered."

What is God saying? Remember means to prepare, to plan, to be ready for the day.

I know my wife would enjoy some roses, some candles maybe, something to eat, going out for a meal, a special event to celebrate our anniversary – that special day.

"Remember" is not merely a mental act. Yes, it recalls the past creation account; but to "remember" is also an activity involving preparation. When God says, "Remember," He wants us to do something about that special memorial. "Remember the Sabbath day to keep it holy." We can *keep* holy only something that has been made holy by a holy God. Now, here we are called upon to keep the Sabbath holy. In Ezekiel 20:12, God goes further and declares that the Sabbath is a sign that He sanctifies His people. The God of love calls us to keep this day holy. And, this day also serves to make God's people holy – to sanctify us.

Appropriate Activities For All

Back to the fourth commandment, in Exodus 20:8-9: "Remember the Sabbath day to keep it holy. Six days you shall labor and do all your work." All "your" work! This implies that the Sabbath is actually for God's "work." That's right. Do your personal labor during the six days of the week, and on the Sabbath you should do God's work.

Now the commandment continues: "But the seventh day is the Sabbath of the LORD your God. In it you shall do no work: you, nor your son, nor your daughter, your male servant, nor your female servant, nor your cattle, nor your stranger who is within your gates. For in six days the LORD made the heavens and earth, the sea, and all that is in them, and rested the seventh day. Therefore the LORD blessed the Sabbath day and hallowed it" (Exodus 20:10-11).

It's a long, inclusive commandment with a special challenge to families, for the commandment includes all "within your gates." In ancient Hebrew times the expression meant within the city gates. Even the foreigners who were not committed Sabbath-keepers were expected to enjoy the blessings of the Sabbath while within the gates. That would have taken some planning, indeed.

Today parents must do some planning to make the Sabbath a delight for all within their "gates." If we work ourselves to exhaustion during the week, making the Sabbath a delight becomes a major challenge. When the weather permitted, Lynda and I took her nephews out to enjoy nature. Although I didn't like going to the smelly dairy barn, Danny loved the cows, so we spent a lot of time at the dairy. Both Danny and Patrick enjoyed the river, so we often cycled along the St. Joseph River.

We must make sure that all within our gates – parents, children, servants, and guests – enjoy the Sabbath.

Probably most of us can say with the well-known empire builder Cecil John Rhodes as he lay dying, "So little done, so much to do." We work, work, work. In His mercy, in His grace, God set aside the Sabbath to remind us that He is the God who redeems us; He is the God who has created us. He wants us to be rejuvenated, refreshed, and renewed every week.

"Sabbath" = Cessation!

What really does the word "Sabbath" mean? Many say: "Rest." However, one Bible commentator says that "the word does *not* mean 'rest,' as has been commonly conjectured." The word actually means "stopping, stoppage, cessation."

I checked my Bible dictionaries, and sure enough, I discovered that the commentator was right. Just as a lawyer who has finished presenting all of the pertinent evidence and arguments says, "I *rest* my case," and just as traditionally we say of one who has just died, "He is *resting* from his labors," even so the Bible records that "God *rested* from His work" (Genesis 2:3). This is not resting up from being tired, but rather, stopping, ending, ceasing what He had been doing. "Resting from" is an important expression. Let's translate it as "cessation from."

The Sabbath is not a day simply to go home and sleep, to stop doing our worldly activities, to stop spending time earning a living. The idea is cessation from our own activities so that we can spend time focusing upon God's activities.

So let's not think of the word "Sabbath" simply as "rest," but rather as ceasing to do our own things so that we can spend time with God.

Exodus 23:12 points out a wonderful effect of Sabbath rest. "Six days you shall do your work, and on the seventh day you shall rest, that your ox and your donkey may rest, and the son of your maidservant and the stranger may be refreshed." Refreshed, renewed, invigorated, energized. Ceasing our work and doing God's work has wonderful effects upon those who keep God's day holy.

The Sabbath refreshes God's people in many ways. Leviticus 23:3 says: "Six days shall work be done, but the seventh day is a Sabbath of solemn rest, a holy convocation" – a time to gather together to worship our Creator and Redeemer. Sabbath is a time of physical, mental, emotional, social, and spiritual refreshing.

Distractions and Distortions

Sadly, there are those who would destroy this sanctuary in time. Some, even believing Christians, have not seen the beauties of this special day of celebration. For example, I discovered the following announcement for 2007: "Evolution Sunday Returns. Hundreds of churches all over the country are going to participate in Evolution Sunday..., to celebrate none other than the 198th birthday of Charles Darwin," the one who said, "I had gradually come by this time [in 1836] to see that the Old Testament from its manifestly false history was no more to be trusted than the sacred books of the Hindus or the beliefs of any barbarian."

Some who reject the seventh-day Sabbath are very honest about it. A well-known Bible commentator says: "There is no commandment in the New Testament inculcating the sacredness of the first day of the week and demanding that Christians observe it scrupulously for holy purposes." Now that's honest!

Some time ago a friend of mine gave me a copy of a magazine called *Our Amazing Week* which reported a study done by a Seventh-day Baptist who had studied hundreds of languages around the world and found out that there are scores of languages which use some form of the word "Sabbath" as the name for the seventh day of the week. For example, Spanish uses the word "sábado."

Also, someone slipped under my door a copy of *The Sentinel,* a journal of St. Catherine's Catholic Church, in Michigan. In the journal was an article written by a Catholic priest, Father Broderick. To check whether or not the article was genuine, I called St. Catherine's and asked: "Is this real? Did Father Broderick write the article?"

"Yes. But he's now retired."

Listen to Father Broderick: "People who think that the Scriptures should be the sole authority should logically become Seventh-day Adventists and keep Saturday holy."

Summons to Sabbath Celebration

I want to make a brief but pointed two-fold challenge here – two basic appeals.

First, to those who already know about and believe in the sanctity of the seventh-day Sabbath: By God's grace, and to His glory, seek for the best way to enjoy this delightful day, both in the preparation, as well as in practice of this special day.

Second, to those who are not keeping God's holy day: Take time to dig deeply into the Scriptures. Read the whole Bible, from Genesis to Revelation, and see how this vital commandment is upheld as a significant requirement for all who love the Lord. Love for the Lord will lead to loyalty to His law regarding the seventh day Sabbath, a day of delight!

Let's plan for this day every week. Let's prepare for it, and celebrate it in the proper manner for God's glory. This guideline for a great life will provide the crucial balance in the hectic lifestyle of the twenty-first century.

"Remember the Sabbath day to keep it holy."

Chapter 5
I Pledge Allegiance . . .

"And God spoke all these words:
'Honor your father and your mother,
that your days may be long
in the land the LORD your God
is giving to you.'"
(Exodus 20:1, 12 NET)

An article in the November 29, 2006, *Boston Herald* reads as follows: "As if liposuction, dimples, Botoxed droopy eyelids ... and dreaded 'trout pout' collagened lips weren't enough, a new survey has found that rampant cosmetic surgery is robbing our country of one of its greatest resources: grandmothers."

Just the month before, a book came out with the title: *Beauty Junkies: Inside Our 15 Billion Dollar Obsession with Cosmetic Surgery.* Fifteen billion! Why all that money? That *Herald* article continues: "Critics attribute the boom in cosmetic surgery to a youth-obsessed culture. Plastic surgery no longer is limited to celebrities." The article talks about various things: nose reshaping, liposuction, tummy tucks, etc. And it's not just women; it's men as well – the percentage of men getting treatments is going up too!

Yet, listen to this: "Despite all the progress, there is no single-dose fountain of youth. Like all cosmetic surgery, many of these procedures are temporary fixes that must be re-administered every few months."

Fifteen billion dollars, and I wonder: Are Americans spending billions upon billions of dollars because we have forgotten something very, very important?

Scripture Support for Seniors

Let's find the answer in Leviticus 19:32. As is clear from a careful reading of the chapter, Leviticus 19 is a reiteration of apparently all of the decalogue, of Exodus 20. Leviticus 19:32 may reveal part of the reason why Americans are spending billions in order to try to recapture the fountain of youth.

Now of course, the setting of this verse is an ancient Israelite society: "You shall rise before the grey headed and honor the presence of an old man, and fear your God. I am the Lord." Or as the New International Version puts it simply: "You shall show respect for the elderly."

Think about that. If our society practiced showing respect for the elderly, I suspect people might even begin to go and try to get cosmetic surgery to look older! To get more respect. But we are so focused, so fixated, upon a youth culture that we're spending 15 billion dollars to look young!

The Commandment that "Connects"

This book deals with the Ten Commandments, the first four of which are generally seen as referring to our relationship with God, and the last six as referring to our human relationships.

Now, for a quick reminder about the number of words in these commandments, as mentioned earlier. In the Hebrew language, the middle commandment – the fourth – has about sixty words. The first three commandments have about sixty words. And the last six commandments have about sixty words. Fascinating! And that's why, in a certain sense, the fourth commandment is smack bang in the middle!

However, there's another way to look at the Ten Commandments. Some have suggested that the fifth commandment, in a sense, is the bridge. The bridge? Yes, because it looks back to "the Lord your God" and it looks forward to the way we treat our parents. So in a sense, it forms a connection. Before we cross that bridge, come with me on a fascinating side trip.

Frequent Focus on the Family

Look at Exodus 20:2, the first commandment. Notice what it says: "I am the Lord your God who brought you out of the land of Egypt." And out of what? "The *house* of bondage." Isn't it interesting that the word "house" is there? And what does the last commandment say? "You shall not covet your neighbor's *house*." I had not noticed that before. The commandments start out with God saying, "I have redeemed you from that house of slavery" – obviously a symbol of sin. Then when we get to the last of the moral laws, we read, "Don't covet somebody else's house. I saved you from a house of slavery."

Now look at the second commandment. In Exodus 20:5, for example, we're told not to bow down to worship false gods because "I the Lord your God am a jealous God" – a God with a love relationship with His people, a God who visits "the iniquity of the fathers upon the children." Implied again is the matter of "family" ties!

In the fourth commandment family members are mentioned: "The seventh day is the Sabbath of the Lord your God. In it you shall do no work: you, nor your son, nor your daughter."

Do you notice what keeps coming up over and over again? Later, we're going to be studying the seventh commandment, which also deals with family issues. What comes up over and over again? Family relationships – one of the institutions of Eden.

This concept of the family is a vital part of the commandments. And that's one of the places the Devil is trying to make his most insidious attacks.

Biblical Balance of Both Parents

"Honor your father and your mother." Let's stop right there. Isn't that interesting? Sometimes people have said, "Oh, the Hebrew culture, the Israelites, they were a patriarchal society." But what does it say? Honor whom? Father and *mother*.

Now let's go to Leviticus 19:3, to see something fascinating: "Every one of you shall revere his mother and his father, and keep My Sabbaths." Isn't that an interesting order? Mother, then father.

Let's return now to Exodus 20: "Honor your father and your mother." Notice, it includes a "father" and a "mother." As one Bible commentator said:"This commandment, the fifth commandment, obviously rules on same sex marriages." I had never realized that before – "your father and your mother." It takes both a *father* and a *mother* to make a family truly, scripturally complete.

Have you heard this saying before? Let's see if you can complete it for me: The hand that rocks the cradle rules what?" Yes, the world. The hand that rocks the cradle rules the world. What does that mean? Mothers have a tremendous impact, make an indelible imprint, have a telling influence upon their children.

Think about Moses for a moment. Why do you think, other than God's obvious great blessing upon him, that Moses had such a great place in the history of this world? Who raised him? His mother. On the positive side we see a great man of God like Moses. On the negative side we can read the sad story of one of the worst men ever to rule this world: Nero. His mother largely made him who he was. Mothers have a great impact on their children. Let's not miss that, because too often we see the Bible or the Old Testament as patriarchal. There's also a balance.

Digging Deeper into the Decalogue

Let's return to the bridge commandment and spend some time reflecting on verse 12. It starts with the word "honor." Let's stop there and consider that word. That word in Hebrew is *kah-veyth*. It actually means "heavy or weighty" compared with "light." In simple terms, "treat with great respect, as something very important, highly prized, something that deserves the honor and the weight with which it comes." The word can also be rendered: "respect, esteem, have regard for, have concern for, have affection for, prize highly."

Consider now, some counsel from the wisest and richest man who ever lived. Among the many passages helping to define the word "honor," I've selected just a couple of passages. Here's an example in Proverbs 1:8: "My son, hear the instruction of your father." By the way, in the Hebrew, when it says "hear" it means "obey." When

Samuel said, "Speak, for Your servant hears" (1 Samuel 3:10), he was not saying, "I'm going to listen to you God and then do my own thing." No, he was saying, "I'm ready to listen and obey."

When a parent asks a child, "Are you listening to me?" what does the parent mean? The child may reply, "Yes, I hear you, Mom." But what does the child mean?

So when the Bible says, "Hear the instruction of your father," it means "follow that instruction; do what your father says". Then Proverbs 1:8 continues: "And do not forsake the law of your mother."

Proverbs 6:20 reiterates the same idea. Using the stronger word "keep," it talks about a father's instruction and a mother's teaching: "My son, keep your father's command, and do not forsake the law of your mother." Now incidentally, many think that the command to honor father and mother applies only to children and teenagers.

Interestingly enough, however, many Bible scholars have looked at this verse and have discovered that the primary emphasis for this fifth commandment is not just for offspring who are infants and youth but for all people of all ages, for all time. That's surprising. This is for adults. The commandment does not say, "Children, honor your father and mother." Rather, it simply says, "Honor your father and your mother" – no age category specified. This calls upon all of us to honor our parents when we're children needing guidance, when we're teens needing advice, when we're adults needing to give assistance, and when we're their successors needing to bring honor to the names of the deceased by the way we live our lives.

Dishonoring Is Disastrous

Just about now some children here might be thinking, "I'm so thankful I didn't live during Old Testament times, because back then dishonoring parents was a very serious matter." Let's see how serious this commandment was during the time of the theocracy. It doesn't say what age they are, but these are children still living at home.

Deuteronomy 27:16 contains some very strong words: "Cursed is the one who treats his father or his mother with contempt." Let's find out what actually happened to people who treated their parents like that – with contempt. Deuteronomy 21:18-21: "If a man has a stubborn and rebellious son who will not obey the voice of his father or the voice of his mother, and who when they have chastened him will not heed them, then his father and his mother shall take hold of him and bring him out to the elders of his city, to the gate of his city, and they shall say to the elders of the city, 'This son of ours is stubborn and rebellious; he will not obey our voice; he is a glutton and a drunkard.' Then all the men of the city shall stone him to death with stones; and so you shall put away the evil from among you, and all Israel shall hear and fear."

Exodus 21:15, 17 and Leviticus 20:9 repeat that "bad" news.

Disobedience Divinely-Directed?

Let's go now to the New Testament, because I know some of you are saying, "Phew, I'm glad I don't live under the theocracy. Let's look at the good news." Ephesians chapter 6 states a serious matter for anybody who is a son or a daughter. Let's go to Ephesians 6:1-4, because here, by inspiration, the great apostle Paul brings to our attention the importance of this commandment. Notice his language: "Children, obey your parents in the Lord."

We need to pause here, because there are times when some parents are not doing the right thing. They're asking their children to do sinful things. If they are saying, "Do this" and they are not in the Lord, should children obey them? No! And the best way to honor parents at that point is by disobeying them – if and when the parents are outside the Lord. For a classic example of this, read 1 Samuel 19 – the story of Saul, who said to his son Jonathan, and his soldiers, "Go kill David." David was not guilty of anything. So, what did Jonathan do? He honored his father by disobeying him! Yes! Jonathan honored by disobeying because Saul was outside of the Lord. Very interesting story!

The Promise of Prosperity

Let's return to Ephesians 6:1-4: "Children, obey your parents in the Lord, for this is right. Honor your father and mother, which is the first commandment with promise." Why? Notice the rest, and this seems to come from the book of Deuteronomy: "That it may be well with you [that is, prosperity] and you may live long on the earth [that is, longevity]." Prosperity and longevity are both going to come our way if we honor and obey those who exert rightful authority.

Look at the rest of the admonition to see what this "rightful" authority may mean: "And you, fathers, do not provoke your children to wrath." So parents, don't cause problems. The Bible is balanced, isn't it?

There's another person who said this in modern language. "The parent who, when correcting a child, gives way to anger is more at fault than the child" (*Child Guidance*, 246). And the reason for that is that children don't so much learn from what we say, but from what we do. It's indeed a high calling.

Let's finish that passage in Ephesians: "And you, fathers, do not provoke your children to wrath, but bring them up in the training and admonition of the Lord." There is the rest of the high calling to parents, a very important call.

So, do you want to have longevity and prosperity? Lots of people do, and so they look in all kinds of places to find these blessings. In January 2007, I found a copy of *USA Today* under the door to my hotel room. I picked it up, opened it, and glanced through it. One article entitled "A Better Life" reported that what young people, especially college students, have as their life's goals are fame and wealth. Those young people, and the rest of us, might do well to notice this quotation from a recent *Time* magazine: "Money can't buy happiness." So according to the author of the *Time* magazine article, where can we find happiness? The writer gave eight rules governing the science of happiness. One of them was to invest time and energy with friends and family.

Problem Youth & the Perfect Pattern

A man once complained, "Youth today love luxury. They have bad manners, contempt for authority, no respect for older people, talk nonsense when they should work. Young people do not stand up any longer when adults enter the room. They contradict their parents. They talk too much in company. They guzzle their food. They ... tyrannize their elders." Sounds like the *USA Today* article mentioned above; but the man who said that was Socrates, who lived about 400 years before Christ.

The above references reveal the validity of the fifth commandment for all time and for all cultures– an eternal principle of God's standard for all people, whether ancient or modern.

Let's go to 2 Timothy 3:1-5, where we'll look at some sad news before we examine some good news. This passage is a caution, a reminder, a reality check: "But know this, that in the last days perilous times will come: for men will be lovers of themselves, lovers of money, boasters, proud, blasphemers, disobedient to parents, unthankful, unholy, unloving, unforgiving, slanderers, without self-control, brutal, despisers of good, traitors, headstrong, haughty, lovers of pleasure rather than lovers of God, having a form of godliness but denying its power. And from such turn away!"

So we know what kind of people we shouldn't follow, including those in these last days who will be "disobedient to parents."

Now let's move to the good news. Whom should we follow? Let's look at the best example ever. Knowing that no person is perfect, let's turn to the only one who lived a perfect life on earth: Jesus. We must encourage all children – no matter what their age – to look to Jesus, the perfect pattern for all of us, as noted in 1 Peter 2:21.

The Model of the Master

The story as in Luke 2 tells of Jesus who went up to Jerusalem with His parents. He remained in the temple there. Even as a twelve-year-old, He understood His calling – a sacred calling, a very high calling. When His parents found Him, He said,

"Why is it that you sought Me? Did you not know that I must be about My Father's business?" (Luke 2:49). He recognized who He was and what He was supposed to do. Yet notice the example He left behind for all of us, in His living out the fifth commandment: "Then he went down with them and came to Nazareth and was subject to them, but his mother kept all these things in her heart. And Jesus increased in wisdom and stature, and in favor with God and man" (verses 51-52). Jesus was submissive to His parents. He is our example. Now, this was when he was a child.

Let's fast forward, towards the end of his life – twenty-some years later. Jesus tearfully confronted the adult religious traditionalist leaders of his day: "Why do you also transgress the commandment of God because of your tradition? For God commanded, saying, 'Honor your father and your mother;' and, 'He who curses father or mother, let him be put to death.' But you say, 'Whoever says to his father or mother, "Whatever profit you might have received from me is a gift to God" – 'then he need not honor his father or mother.' Thus you make the commandment of God of no effect by your tradition" (Matthew 15:3-6). These adult leaders were looking for excuses. They didn't want to take care of their parents. But this commandment is not just for young children, as noted above – it's for all of us, all the way through our lives.

Finally, we see Jesus as an adult hanging on the cross. The Scripture records: "Seeing his mother, with the disciple whom he loved standing beside her, Jesus said to her, 'Mother, there is your son'; and to the disciple, 'There is your mother'; and from that moment the disciple took her into his house"

(John 19:26-27 REB). Jesus, even as he was dying, honored his mother.

Putting the Principle into Practice

I'll end with a short story. My wife Lynda and I spent four years as missionaries in Zimbabwe. I was a teacher, and also had the privilege of preaching often. Even the week before we were supposed to leave, I preached at Camp Meeting.

One day, a local farmer came over to me and said: "I've heard several of your sermons and I have been blessed by them, but I liked best the message you and your wife preached by example." What was he talking about?

My parents, far from being wealthy, had raised their own children and then, when my sister died, they'd spent lots of time, energy, and money raising three grandchildren. Lynda and I had decided that, before returning to the United States, we should give my parents a parting gift, so we gave them my car.

This was what had prompted that farmer to say: "More than any sermon I have ever heard you preach, what you just did for your parents preaches more loudly than what you have said."

It's not simply what we say. It's how we treat our parents that matters most. And it's not just parents. It's actually anyone in authority. Ephesians chapter 6 points that out. Also, 1 Peter 2 calls for us to "honor the king" – anyone who is in authority, so long as they don't go against what God calls upon us to do.

All of us, no matter what age, need to be faithful in treating those in authority with respect, and our parents with the honor they deserve – no matter how they treat us – because they've been placed in that position. Let's be like David when he treated Saul with respect, even though Saul didn't deserve it. (See 2 Samuel 26).

Even though some of our parents and leaders may not be godly people, let's pledge our full allegiance to them, as long as they do not call on us to diminish God's sovereignty and authority in our lives. As Scripture notes, if we lovingly and loyally follow this guideline for a great life, we will be blessed with a long and prosperous life!

Chapter 6
Guy Fawkes & Grave Diggers

"And God spoke all these words:
'You shall not kill.'"
(Exodus 20:1, 13 NET)

Having been raised in South Africa, I got to know about Guy Fawkes Day. Guy Fawkes Day was a special time for all of us kids. As we were growing up, we looked forward to celebrating that day. Yes, it was a holiday – an exciting time when we set off fireworks – something like the Fourth of July in the USA. It was really a fun time! Later I learned the story behind the celebration. On November 6, 1606, because he was unhappy with the leadership in England, Guy Fawkes led a group who tried to blow up the Parliament building and the people in it, including King James I.

Since South Africa was once a British colony and eventually part of the Commonwealth, we celebrated Guy Fawkes Day with fireworks – celebrating the fact that Guy Fawkes did not get his fireworks to work. The Parliament building was not blown up because the plot was discovered just in time – something worth celebrating: the saving of human life, not the taking of it.

The sixth commandment in the King James Version reads: "Thou shalt not kill." As we open our Bibles and spend a little time studying this commandment, somebody might be thinking, "But Pastor, I don't kill people."

Yes, but still the Bible has some practical counsel for all of us. So, let's go to our Bibles.

Confusion Over the Commandment

Again today, I'm using the New King James Version, which I've been using throughout our study of the Ten Commandments. Here Exodus 20:13, reads: "You shall not murder." Now before we move on, I want to spend a few moments on an intriguing question: Is this translation in the New King James Version correct? Or is the King James Version correct? Debate over which translation is better has gone on for a long time. So which is it: "Thou shalt not kill" or "You shall not murder"?

Interestingly enough, you can go to the Andrews University library and check out various books that deal with this commandment. Some time ago, when I was studying the issue of killing, I noticed something strange: One book stated that the key Hebrew word used in this commandment was *murr*, which allegedly should be rendered "to murder," rather than "to kill" a person. A second book said the Hebrew word in this commandment is *qatal*. A third book claimed that the verb is *ratsach*. Which is it? Rather than going to other books, the best thing to do is to go to the Word of God itself, and to study the term in context.

I have a preacher friend who is very well known globally. I'll give him the name Dr. Jones. If you were to ask Dr. Jones, "Now, what does that word in the sixth commandment mean?" he would reply, "Oh, look at Matthew 19:18." So let's turn there in our Bibles. Dr. Jones says, "How do we know whether it means *murder* or *kill*? Read these words in the King James Version: 'He said to him, "Which?" Jesus said, "Thou shalt do no murder."'"

Dr. Jones concludes: "You see, Jesus says that the word is murder."

Ah, very interesting! Well, let's look at the New American Bible, and see what Jesus says, as translated in this version: "'Which ones?' he asked. Jesus replied, 'You shall not *kill*.'"

Whether he did so consciously or not, my preacher friend chose a Bible version that supported his view. So, he concluded: "Jesus says the sixth commandment refers to *murder*." Now, I've just read from the New American Bible, that Jesus says the sixth commandment refers to *killing*.

Wait a minute. Which one is it? That's not the way to dig into God's Word. Don't use a translation that simply supports what you already believe.

Concepts in Context Bring Clarity

In order to properly understand what a word means, you need to know its context. So let's look at the context for the word translated by some as "murder" and by others as "kill."

Go to Deuteronomy 4. I want to show you that the Bible has these words in a definite context. Personally, I began a study of the word in its biblical context some twenty years ago, when still a student at Andrews University. One of my professors had written a paper on this commandment, but it was never published. I got a copy of that paper, and since then have been digging into this issue, and studying it.

If we look at the contextual manner in which words are used, we can see more clearly what these words mean. Deuteronomy 4 is a classic example. This is the chapter immediately before the Ten Commandments, as reiterated by Moses.

Deuteronomy 4:41-42 reads, "Then Moses set apart three cities on this side of the Jordan, toward the rising of the sun, that the manslayer might flee there, who kills...." All English Bible versions use the words "who kills" in this passage.

Stop there. That word "kills" in the Hebrew is *ratsach,* the same word in the sixth commandment. And it says, "who *kills* his neighbor unintentionally, without having hated him in time past, and that by fleeing to one of these cities he might live."

The word *ratsach* appears a total of forty-seven times in the entire Old Testament. Most often the context shows the meaning to be an accidental, unintentional taking of human life done without malice; while less often it is used for premeditated killing, what we normally refer to as "murder." So, we know that this word is a broad term, and therefore it covers a lot. Thus, the sixth commandment cannot be limited simply to murder.

One Bible commentary aptly notes: "*Ratsach* in the sixth commandment is an act of killing, premeditated or not, related to vengeance or not, that violates the standard of living that Yahweh expects of those who have given themselves to Him." Very clear. And Bible commentators repeatedly recognize that concept. It comes up over and over again.

The 2001 New English Translation is helpful here. This translation, with more than 75,000 footnotes, indicates why the translators chose the English terms they did as they translated the Bible.

Listen to how it renders Exodus 20:13, "You shall not kill." The footnote for the Hebrew word *ratsach* used in the sixth commandment reads: "The verb *ratsach* refers to the premeditated or accidental taking of the life of another human being." By the way, this Hebrew term doesn't refer to animals. It's not dealing with the sacrificial system. Then, they finish the footnote as follows: "This commandment teaches the sanctity of all human life." Translators of this modern English version of the Bible have gone back carefully and rightly identified the meaning of the original Hebrew language.

Made in the Maker's Image

Just now you probably have in mind questions which need answers, but questions we won't have time to answer fully here: "What about capital punishment? What about war? What about killing in self-defense? What about abortion?" Although we won't have time to go into all those, we'll begin to get some biblical direction by asking, "Why is life so sacred?"

Genesis 1:26-27: "Then God said, 'Let us make man in Our image, according to Our likeness; let them have dominion over the fish of the sea, over the birds of the air, and over the cattle, over all the earth and over every creeping thing that creeps on the earth.' So God created man in His own image; in the image of God He created him; male and female He created them."

Why is life sacred? Simple reason: We are created in God's image. That's right. And that's why, as the New English Translation has pointed out, human life is sacred in God's sight. We have been created in God's image. Now again, this is just to whet your appetite. The best translation of the Hebrew word *ratsach* is therefore, "Do not kill."

The Deity and the Death Penalty

What about capital punishment? This is a challenging matter to consider. For it appears that during the time of the theocracy, when God worked through a special group of people, He did call upon these Israelites to practice what we call capital punishment – the death penalty. But you know what's interesting? This word *ratsach* used in the sixth commandment is not used for capital punishment. It's a different term, a different concept.   Now here's my hypothetical question: If while God was in direct charge of His people, and let's say He had made a mistake (which we know He never did), but if God had made a mistake and had said, "That person is guilty. He should be executed" and later found that He had made a mistake, then God could have resurrected those who had been executed – brought them back to life.

But What About War?

During Old Testament times, the Israelites were involved in warfare. Significantly, this word *ratsach* is not used in the Bible in connection with war.

While Israel was under theocratic rule, God at times sent the Israelites to carry out some of His tasks, involving destruction of a nation through warfare. Today, however, we do not live under a theocracy.

Interestingly enough, during his April 2006 "Let's Talk" session in South America, the president of the General Conference of Seventh-day Adventists, Dr. Jan Paulsen, stated: "From the very beginning, Seventh-day Adventists have been opposed to war. One of its earliest General Conference sessions (1867) voted the statement that 'the bearing of arms, or engaging in war, is a direct violation of the teachings of our Saviour, and of the spirit and letter of the law of God.'

"In other words, war is a tragic distortion of God's plan for His creation, and Adventists cannot support such violence. As a result, Adventists are 'compelled to decline all participation in acts of war and bloodshed as being inconsistent with the duties enjoined upon us by our divine Master toward our enemies and toward all mankind.'"

Recently, I asked a friend of mine: "How are your sons doing?"

"Well, my one son has never chosen to become baptized. He has now decided to enter the military."

This son was raised in an Adventist home and went to Adventist schools, so I asked the father, "What is required of your son in the military?"

"When you join the military voluntarily, the armed forces make no concessions regarding the seventh-day Sabbath. Sabbath is treated like every other day. It is impossible to join the military and keep the Sabbath." And, this is not even addressing about the matter of taking up arms?

Incidentally, what about military chaplains? At the May 20, 1943, Spring Meeting of the General Conference committee (convening in New York), the following statement was voted: "Military chaplains are ministers of religion to the men in the armed forces. They are employed by the government and are remunerated from public funds for the teaching of religion. This is a practice which is in clear violation of biblical principles concerning the separation of church and state." Interesting! But clearly a Bible-based concept.

Confirming the official view of the church, the Biblical Research Institute, in its October 2003 *Reflections* Newsletter, shared this information: "The Adventist Church is not abandoning its advocacy of noncombatancy. On the contrary! It invites all church members to follow Christ's footsteps and live according to the Sermon on the Mount." A high, Christlike standard!

Defending Life with Death

Often people come to me and say, "But Ron, let's get to the point. If somebody breaks into your home, intent on attacking you and your wife, what are you going to do?"

My answer: "By God's grace, and through His power, I hope that I have the words, the concepts, the very thinking of Jesus so flooding my soul that I can respond with what the Lord has already called upon me to do."

Luke 6:27-28 records these words of Jesus: "But I say to you...." Jesus says to do what? To kill your enemies? What does he say? "Love your enemies, do good to those who hate you, bless those who curse you, and pray for those who spitefully use you." An impossibility?

Here's just one story of someone who put that basic principle of selfless love into action. Her name was Maggie Ferris, and she lived in Philadelphia. One evening Maggie was walking down a main street, minding her own business. Suddenly, out of nowhere, a guy came behind her and put a knife to her throat. Maggie had already put into her mind that she must love her enemy, in practical terms. Her immediate natural instinct was to do something to protect herself, but then she realized that the man holding the knife was a desperate individual who urgently needed help. So what did she do? She didn't fight, she didn't struggle. She said, "Listen, we're on a main street. We'd better go down a side street. We don't want to cause any more problems."

"Huh? What?"

"Let's get off the main street so we won't cause any more problems."

Maggie's concern was for others, not herself. So she took control of the situation. The man obeyed her and went down the side street. Maggie understood human nature as well. There, with a knife to her throat, she kindly said, "You must have had some real serious struggles in your life."

The man put down his knife. Maggie found out that he was a Vietnam veteran, destitute and desperate. And there, on that side street, Maggie began to reach out to this despairing man. By that time, it was getting rather late. Maggie then turned to this hurting human being and said, "Listen, it's late. Would you do me a favor and walk me home?" She saw here a hopeless soul in need of help. The man walked her home, said "Thank you," and left.

The next day Maggie found a bunch of flowers at her door with a note that said, "No one has ever treated me this way before."

I'm not saying that we should put ourselves in harm's way. Don't be presumptuous. My point is this: Wouldn't it be wonderful if anytime we were in a situation where our lives were threatened by some hopeless person, we could think of that person as a soul to be saved? Wouldn't that be great? That's what we're talking about. Life is precious.

Yes, I am aware that it is a legal right in many countries to kill in self-defense. However, we are not talking about the codes of a country; we are considering what God's Word calls upon us to do. And, read in its proper context, there is no passage in Scripture that supports the idea of killing another human being in self-defense. On the contrary, the Christian's call is one of self-sacrificial love.

Think about it. Too many times we've accepted the humanistic belief that life, this life, is all we have. No, there is a life beyond. We need to rethink things, because at times we have been so immersed in cultural concepts, that we have forgotten the higher calling of Jesus Christ. We must think of others and their eternal salvation.

The Preborn and the Reborn

There are many additional questions related to the sixth commandment, including questions about abortion, suicide, and euthanasia. We don't have time to discuss them all here.

Perhaps, a short story can illustrate the matter of abortion. Many are aware that abortion first became legal in the United States through a supreme court ruling called "Roe vs. Wade." Only more recently has it been revealed that the pseudonym "Jane Roe" was used by Norma McCorvey, who was strongly pro-abortion, and worked for years at an abortion clinic.

Norma has changed, given up her previous views, and now has a ministry called "Roe No More." Why? Because her heart was touched by seven-year-old Emily, a kid who would come up and hug her, and say, "I love you, Norma. I don't like what you do to these preborn babies; but I love you." That seven-year-old was the daughter of people involved in Operation Rescue – radical anti-abortion folks, who at times seem to go overboard in an effort to protect the unborn. But this little girl gave Norma hugs and loving words day in and day out.

And Norma McCorvey's reaction? "You know what? I didn't get far in education. I finished the ninth grade. But you know what changed my heart? Emily's blatant affection, frequent hugs, and direct pursuit disarmed me." The little girl's interest was all the more surprising considering that "Emily made it very clear that her acceptance of me wasn't an acceptance of my lifestyle," that is of being actively involved in supporting and promoting abortion. "Early on in our relationship I explained to Emily, 'I like kids and I wouldn't let anyone hurt little kids.' Emily responded, 'Then why do you let them kill the babies in the clinic?'"

Abortion.

Norma McCorvey says, "I wasn't won over by compelling apologetics – biblical arguments. I had a ninth-grade education and a very soft heart. While Operation Rescue adults targeted my mind, Emily went straight to my heart."

Need we say more?

Suicide – Sudden or Slow?

Let's get just a bit more personal here. The title of this chapter? "Guy Fawkes and Grave Diggers." Thus far, we've been dealing with the "Guy Fawkes" part – issues related to taking the lives of other human beings. Now just a brief reflection on "Grave Diggers." Why "grave diggers?" Because Governor Mike Huckabee has a book called *Digging Your Grave With Your Knife and Fork.* Digging your grave with your knife and fork? How so?

There are various ways we can *kill* ourselves. From its biblical context it is clear that the sixth commandment also includes "Do not kill yourself." Yes, it includes suicide. We are made in God's image, so obviously we are not to kill ourselves. The apostle Paul puts it this way: "Do you not know that you are the temple of God and that the Spirit of God dwells in you? If anyone destroys the temple of God, God will destroy him. For the temple of God is holy, which temple you are" (1 Corinthians 3:16-17).

I know the topic of suicide is a difficult and sensitive matter. Suicide is a terrible thing. Even an outstanding Bible character like Elijah for a time seemed somewhat suicidal. He told God that life was not worth living. But guess what? He was stalled from taking his own life by his talking to the Lord (1 Kings 19). Similarly, when Jonah was unhappy with life, he kept talking to the Lord (Jonah 4). So when life is difficult, make sure you talk to the Lord. Keep that communication going.

Suicide can be either sudden or long-term.

Some people smoke themselves to death over a twenty-year period. Other people follow Governor Mike Huckabee's description of a lifestyle of "digging your grave with your fork and your knife," through intemperate diets, sleep habits, etc.

So when the commandment says "Do not kill," let's translate it positively to say, "Live for the Lord in every area of your life!"

Murder Is a Matter of Motives

As with all other activities, this matter of killing all starts in the heart. Genesis 4:5 says, "Cain was very angry" with his brother Abel. When we get to verse 8, it says Cain killed him.

In Matthew 5:22, Jesus cautions us that killing is not simply an act: "But I say to you, that whoever is angry with his brother without a cause shall be in danger of the judgment. And whoever says to his brother, 'Raca!' [that is, you empty head] shall be in danger of the council. But whoever says, 'You fool!' shall be in danger of hell fire."

So when we look at the whole issue, we see that anger begins in the heart, and eventually ends up in action – in killing people.

When W-O-R-D-S Become S-W-O-R-D

This killing, by the way, can even be done through the use of our very communication.

The psalmist says that words can be like a sword– wielded to kill people. We may pat ourselves on the back and say, "Oh, I don't kill people." But Psalm 64:3 speaks of those "who sharpen their tongues like a sword. And bend their bows to shoot their arrows". Those are "bitter words."

In a sense, the words we use on other people can be the swords and arrows that kill them. And so the question I want to ask is this: When we look at the sixth commandment and take it seriously, doesn't it start in the heart? And what the heart is full of overflows from the mouth. We know that.

How do we respond when people say hurtful things about us – gossip about us, do unkind things to us? Do we get angry and say, "I'm going to get even!"? That's the part of the issue we're talking about here. Those words "Do not kill" mean "Love even the people that despitefully use you." Those are the words of Jesus – a very strong challenge, indeed.

Guideline for a Great LIFE!

Let us end with the words of Jesus. May His words inspire us to be peacemakers, to be promoters of life. In John 8:44, we find Jesus reminding us that "Satan was a murderer from the beginning." But Jesus came to give us life. Listen to what He says in John 10:10: "The thief does not come except to steal, and to kill, and to destroy. I have come that they may have life, and that they may have it more abundantly." That's what Jesus wants to give us. He wants each of us to have an abundant life, a wonderful life, a fruitful life, a beneficial life, a healthy life; but not just a life here on this earth.

Jesus wants us to have everlasting life. He says, "Be thou faithful unto death, and I will give you the crown of life" (Revelation 2:10).

Live life at its best; plan for eternal life with Jesus! Now that's a *guideline for a great life*!

Chapter 7
Blinders & Burglar Bars

"And God spoke all these words, saying:
'You shall not commit adultery.'"
(Exodus 20:1, 14 NKJV)

A few years ago, I took a group of students from Solusi University in Zimbabwe to the famous waterfall called Victoria Falls. We cycled all the way there from Bulawayo – 270 miles, in two and a half days. We went, not simply for fun. We were on a mission trip.

When we got there, we met with the mayor of the town. After he had welcomed us, he said, "You know what? Victoria Falls is considered one of the seven wonders of the world. But, what you young people have done is the eighth wonder of the world."

Now what had we done? A group of about twenty of us had cycled from Bulawayo all the way to Victoria Falls to promote abstinence. "The eighth wonder of the world". Why? Because, with AIDS being such a huge problem in Africa, these youth were promoting abstinence from sex outside of marriage and from recreational drugs as the best protection against HIV/AIDS. It is becoming more and more recognized that the mechanical protection devices so widely promoted do not always work. The scientific literature out there says that between fifteen to thirty-some percent of so-called protection devices fail to give protection from infection. Using such devices is like playing Russian roulette. AIDS is just a slower way to die.

Medieval Church & Marital Change

Because God wants us to live healthy, happy, harmonious, and holy lives, He has given us guidelines for a great life.

Exodus 20:14 declares: "You shall not commit adultery." The Hebrew word *na'aph* (to commit adultery) is a verb that can be applied to both male and female, to men and to women.

We'll take some time to unpack this brief law here. But, we'll also seek to avoid the extremes, such as that of some religious leaders during medieval church times. I've read that, in trying to protect marriage, these church leaders created many holy days during which people could not have conjugal relationships with their spouses. Can you guess how many holy days they came up with eventually? One hundred and eighty-three! So, for more than half of the year you were restricted from enjoying the special relationship that the Lord set aside for husbands and wives.

Then along came the Protestant Reformation. Probably some of you are saying, "Praise the Lord!" The Reformation turned things upside down– turned us back to the Bible, back to the biblical concept of what God has provided for us.

Created for Close Companionship

Why is this commandment so important? Why did God set up the marriage relationship? In Genesis chapter 1 we read of God pronouncing each day's creative activities good. But in Genesis 2:18 God says, "It is *not* good that man should be alone. I will make him a helper comparable to him."

Verse 21: "And the Lord God caused a deep sleep to fall on Adam and he slept and He took one of his ribs and closed up the flesh in its place. Then the rib which the Lord God had taken from the man He made into a woman, and He brought her to the man." Incidentally, based on the Hebrew language, another way to say "He made into a woman," is "He architecturally designed the woman."

Then, God brought her to the man. And Adam said, "This is now bone of my bones, and flesh of my flesh. She shall be called woman because she was taken out of man." Finally, verse 24: "Therefore a man shall leave his father and mother and be joined to his wife, and they shall become one flesh." This is God's plan and purpose for marital unity!

Distortions of the Divine Design

That was Genesis 2. Now I'd like to take you on a quick survey through just part of the book of Genesis. You will notice how rapidly human beings began to pervert the beautiful plan that God set up. God was the one to perform a marriage ceremony. He instituted marriage, established it.

1. Polygamy

Yet, by the time we get to Genesis 4, we find marriage tarnished by Lamech (not the Lamech who was the father of Noah, but another Lamech through the line of Cain). Lamech introduced polygamy by marrying two wives. As recognized by various Old Testament scholars, part of the reason for the flood, was the polygamous marriages of these peoples.

Some time ago I had the opportunity of looking into the issue of polygamy in depth, through the research done for my doctoral study at Andrews

University. As a product of my study I wrote *Polygamy in the Bible*. Many people seem to misunderstand this issue in Scripture. As a result, some are going down a divergent path, trying to promote strange things, such as allowing the practice of polygamy within the church!

Dr. Richard Davidson, the chair of the Old Testament department at Andrews University, has recently completed a book about sexuality in the Old Testament, *Flame of Yahweh*, which includes the topic of polygamy. Davidson's careful biblical research corroborates my own doctoral research, that God never tolerated polygamy. Actually, Scripture reveals that polygamy was outlawed. Many haven't dug deeply enough into the Word of God to see that God was completely against polygamy. Yes, even some of the so called "faithful" went against it – Abraham, David, Jacob, Solomon. But careful study reveals that God brought judgments upon them, they went through reconversions, quit their polygamy, and took care of the women and children.

2. Inter-Faith

Fast forward to Genesis 6 where we read the well-known story of the flood. Here it says, "And the sons of God saw the daughters of men that they were beautiful" (verse 2). This is the issue of what we call inter-faith marriages. In Genesis 6 we find that God also placed judgments upon those who intermarried with unbelievers.

Both polygamy and inter-faith marriages deviate from God's original, ideal plan for families.

3. Homosexuality

Over time people began going further away from God. Genesis 19 presents the well-known story of Sodom and Gomorrah. Among other problems in these two towns a major one was obviously the issue of homosexuality. The result? Both cities were supernaturally destroyed as a judgment from God.

4. Rape

Genesis 34:2 presents another problem that occurs as people move away from God's ideal. I'll read just one verse: "When Shechem the son of Hamor the Hivite, prince of the country, saw her [i.e., Dinah], he took her and lay with her, and violated her." So here is sexual molestation and violation.

5. Incest

In Genesis 35 we find an incestuous relationship between Reuben and Bilhah. All this, in just the first 35 chapters of the book of Genesis. Over and over again we find people moving away from God's ideal for us.

Death Due to Disobedience

The Bible has lots of counsel and guidance on marital issues. Some vital principles can be gleaned from chapters such as Exodus 22; Leviticus 18, 20, and 21; Deuteronomy 10, and 22 through 27. God was giving guidelines for His people so they would know how to live in the joy that God has established for a proper, loving, conjugal relationship.

Look at Deuteronomy 22:22 as an example of how serious this marriage issue is. To go against the pattern, the plan, the norm that God has established is serious business. Notice what was to happen in ancient Israel during the time of the theocracy: "If a man is found lying with a woman married to a husband, then both of them shall die." Both of them shall die – death penalty for the violation of this commandment. It was serious business – and still is!

Today the results are actually similar. Not that we live under a theocracy, but we suffer the results ourselves – disease, and even death.

Some of my own friends, friends I went to school with, Christians, even leaders in the church, have suffered the consequences of violating these biblically-established family moral standards.

I'll never forget. My wife Lynda and I went traveling. We picked up an unmarried youth leader in Johannesburg and drove together down to Cape Town, South Africa. Within a few weeks, we heard that she had died. From what? AIDS. And that's not because she got it from a blood transfusion, if you know what I mean. The other young lady was also single – an elementary church school teacher. She too died of AIDS. She had been a very dear friend of mine. Why these tragic deaths? In literal terms, even in today's world, sin brings death.

The Culture of Cohabitation

Let's go back to 1960 in the USA, before the so-called cultural-social revolution, and look at some statistics. In 1960 seven percent, that is, about 1 out of 13 or 14, of American children were born out of wedlock, what we call illegitimate children. By 2002 the percentage had moved from seven to thirty-three percent. Abortion was not legal in 1960. So, even with about 1,300,000 abortions per year we still have thirty-three percent of babies born outside of marriage.

Where has society gone? Where are we headed? We older ones need not get into a huff and say, "Oh, these young people!" The journal for the American Association of Retired People published an article entitled "Unmarried Together" which reports that more than 260,000 unmarried Americans aged sixty-five and older are living together – to say nothing of another almost five million other Americans who do the same thing. All, of course, going against this beautiful marriage institution that God set up.

Currently, of all Americans that get married, two-thirds sexually cohabited before marriage. Somebody may say, "Yeah but, you know, before you buy a car, you've got to take it for a test drive! Right?" That's what seems to be happening in society, and even within Christian communities. People "lease" partners for a year or two and then trade them back in as used goods. This is bad news! For, according to a 2005 NBC report, those who live together before marriage are twice as likely to divorce as those who do not live together before marriage.

Here's another unhappy statistic. Couples who simply live together experience five times the number of incidents of severe violence as do those who are married.

Mind Manipulation by the Media

The evidence is clear, but the devil is constantly bombarding.

A few years ago I was watching a recording of a good program which was interrupted by a commercial by a well-known actress. First, the well-dressed actress introduced the product. In the next scene the actress' dress had come down on her shoulder. By the third scene the dress had dropped seductively low. At first I was puzzled about what was happening. But a bit of reflection made me aware that the advertisers were subtly trying to seduce the audience into continuing to watch so that the viewers would buy the advertised product.

Satan is present in romance novels, in books, in videos, on TV, on the internet – you name it. In the United States the average American is bombarded with 10,000 sensual messages per year through television alone – 10,000 messages demonically designed to lead us astray from divine delights.

What about music? Some of us can remember the subtle innuendos in the words of songs sung twenty or thirty years ago. Today the words of popular songs are no longer subtle. Someone observed that today even if you can't understand the words, you still get the message by what you see and feel.

A study published in 2006 reported that teens, of both genders and all races, who listen to music with sexually-blatant themes are more likely to be sexually promiscuous. By beholding we become changed.

Concerned families whose teens have iPods can hardly monitor what those teens are downloading and listening to. Satan, that roaring lion, is devouring many who choose to listen to these degrading songs.

Solution for Sexual Sin? "Surgery"!

The devil is very clever. He has traps set for all of us, no matter our age, gender, ethnicity, profession, education, or social position. He starts with our hearts, our minds.

And that's where Jesus starts also. Jesus cautions us, calls us to a higher standard. He warns us, because He knows that it all starts in the mind, in the heart.

Let's look at the words of Jesus in that famous Sermon on the Mount. Matthew 5:27: "You have heard that it was said to those of old, 'You shall not commit adultery.'" Apparently, some seemed to limit adultery to only the act. Verse 28: "But I say to you that whoever looks at a woman to lust for her has already committed adultery with her in his heart." Very interesting.

Let's make a tangent to Matthew 15 and then return to Matthew 5. In both texts Jesus speaks on similar themes. Matthew 15:19: "For out of the heart proceed evil thoughts [that's where it all starts], murders, adulteries, fornications, thefts, false witness, blasphemies."

Back to Matthew chapter 5, where Jesus tells us what we need to do if our hearts are going astray. Jesus calls for radical surgery. Notice verse 29: "If your right eye causes you to sin, pluck it out and cast it from you; for it is more profitable for you that one of your members perish, than for your whole body to be cast into hell."

Now to verse 30: "And if your right hand causes you to sin, cut it off and cast it from you; for it is more profitable for you that one of your members perish, than for your whole body to be cast into hell."

Some may have heard of Aron Ralston, the young man who got his right arm caught under an eight-hundred-pound boulder. He suffered there for about five days, with virtually no food or water. Aron realized if he didn't do something radical, he was going to die. Eventually, he broke his arm in two places and then cut it off so that he could survive. And he did survive to tell the story.

Jesus says the issue of the heart being drawn astray is very serious. Now, Jesus is not saying literally to cut your arm off. He's talking about the issue of the heart, of motives, desires. Jesus warns us to not go in any sexually dangerous direction.

Language Laced with Lust

Ephesians 5:3-4 cautions us against our sometimes unintentional involvement in certain ways of speaking. We start sharing innuendos. We start saying things ambiguously. We start getting into areas where the mind is going astray and our words are leading us and others astray.

Notice what inspiration says in Ephesians 5:3-4: "But fornication and all uncleanness or covetousness, let it not even be named among you [i.e., don't even talk about this among yourselves], as is fitting for saints; neither filthiness, nor foolish talking, nor coarse jesting, which are not fitting, but rather giving of thanks."

Pardon for the Promiscuous

It's very important for us to keep away from anything that is not pure, for such things lead us down a path to grievous sin. So what does Paul encourage us to do? 1 Corinthians 6:18-20: "Flee sexual immorality. Every sin that a man does is outside the body, but he who commits sexual immorality sins against his own body. Or do you not know that your body is the temple of the Holy Spirit who is in you, whom you have from God, and you are not your own? For you were bought at a price;

therefore glorify God in your body and in your spirit which are God's."

The reason we need to follow this beautiful seventh commandment is that we have been bought with a price. What price? The blood of Jesus. That's right: the blood of Jesus. In fact, when we go back to the story of David's repentance in Psalm 51, we hear David pray: "Purge me with hyssop." Hyssop, as mentioned in Exodus 12, was the branch that was used to put blood on the lintel and doorposts just before the Israelites left Egypt. They took a hyssop branch and dipped it in the blood of a slain lamb, representing Jesus Christ. "Purge me with hyssop." What beautiful symbolism. Purge me with the blood of Jesus Christ.

That's the good news. God can forgive. God will forgive. God does forgive the violation of the seventh commandment. Even though, as Paul says, it's a sin against your own body, God is willing to forgive. And David says, "Purge me with hyssop and I shall be clean." That's right. Because we've been bought with a price, we can be purged, made clean.

Adultery, sexual immorality, is a serious matter! But there is good news: God is a merciful, forgiving Heavenly Father. "If we confess our sins, He is faithful and just to forgive us our sins and to cleanse us from all unrighteousness" (1 John 1:9).

Judged or Justified by Jesus

John 8:1-11 records a story of a woman caught in the act of adultery. Jesus had said to the woman's accusers: "'He who is without sin among you, let him throw a stone at her first'.... When Jesus had raised Himself up and saw no one but the woman,

He said to her. 'Woman, where are those accusers of yours? Has no one condemned you?' She said, 'No one, Lord.' And Jesus said to her. 'Neither do I condemn you; go and sin no more.'"

Yes, Jesus recognizes it as sin; but He is willing to forgive, to justify us; and, not just forgive but also bid us to stop committing that sin.

We are reminded in 1 Corinthians 6:8-10 that sin is serious business: "Do you not know that the unrighteous will not inherit the kingdom of God? Do not be deceived. Neither fornicators, nor idolaters, nor adulterers, nor homosexuals, nor sodomites, nor thieves, [then the message goes straight to the heart] nor covetous, nor drunkards, nor revilers, nor extortioners will inherit the kingdom of God."

This is a very serious matter, for these are the people who will not be with Jesus Christ for eternity. But verse 11 gives us good news: "And such were some of you." Did you notice the word "were"? What does that mean? It's past. They have been forgiven. And "such were some of you."

By the way, this puts a lie to the theory "once an alcoholic, always an alcoholic," or "once a homosexual, always a homosexual." No. "Such *were* some of you. But you were washed, but you were sanctified, but you were justified in the name of the Lord Jesus Christ and by the Spirit of our God." Here is the forgiveness that God offers to anybody who wants it.

Persistently Protect the Portals

Martin Luther, who helped get rid of the medieval church's 183 days of conjugal prohibition for married couples, wrote as follows about the seventh commandment: "This commandment applies to every form of unchastity.... Your heart, your lips, your whole body are to be chaste and to afford no occasion, aid, or encouragement to unchastity."

Luther, who took part in getting rid of man-made restrictions and changing things back to biblical standards, still cautioned us not to become entrapped by the devil's temptations to violate this commandment in any way, shape or form.

In the twenty-first century, it is crystal clear that the devil is actively going about "like a roaring lion, seeking whom he may devour" (1 Peter 5:8). Which is why the Scripture warns all to "Be sober and alert" (1 Peter 5:8 NET), and to "resist him" (verse 9).

People who live in dangerous areas often have burglar bars installed in order to keep out intruders. While these protective bars may help to keep sexual predators out, the devil is still able to seduce people within their own homes – through sensuality in the media. Therefore, we need to have the Lord equip us with a set of "spiritual" blinders, so that we will be able to keep "our eyes on Jesus, on whom our faith depends from start to finish" (Hebrews 12:2 NLT).

How should we guard our hearts? Philippians 4:8 notes: "Finally, brethren, whatever things are true, whatever things are noble, whatever things are just, whatever things are pure, whatever things are lovely, whatever things are of good report, if there is any virtue and if there is anything praiseworthy – meditate on these things." This *guideline for a great life* is a guarantee for success in this life and in the future.

Chapter 8
Is It Just Fuzzy Math?

"And God spoke all these words, saying:
'You shall not steal.'"
(Exodus 20:1, 15 NKJV)

Five hijackers stopped a man at gun point and tried to steal the victim's car. One of the hijackers was sitting in their own car while the four others came around the victim's car. The victim got out because there was a gun pointed at him. As he got out, he took his car keys with him. He managed to push two of the hijackers away and rush over to their car, catch them by surprise, pull the driver out of their car, and jump into their car and drive off, with his keys with him. And where did he drive? Straight to the police station, where he reported the attempted hijacking. In short order guess who showed up – the hijackers claiming their car had been stolen – stolen by the man whose car they were trying to hijack! Of course, they were promptly arrested.

You might smile at this story, but it's interesting how sometimes unusual things happen to us when we try to do things to other people.

Statistics on Stealing

The 2007 *Guinness Book of World Records* has some interesting statistics regarding crime in the world. It's fascinating, yet sad, that of the seven crimes listed, five of them deal with stealing:

- Robberies: The highest of any country is Spain – almost half a million robberies.
- Kidnappings: The top country in the world is Colombia – more than 5,000 kidnappings.
- Fraud: Germany leads the world with almost 900,000 cases of fraud.
- Car thefts: The United States leads, with over a million car thefts and burglaries.

As we observe the statistics, it becomes obvious that we need to take time to seriously study the eighth commandment, which reads: "Thou shalt not steal" (Exodus 20:15).

The Scope of "Stealing"

What does this commandment cover? What is its scope, according to the Bible?

Let's begin by considering Exodus 21:16: "He who kidnaps a man and sells him, or if he is found in his hand, shall surely be put to death." Kidnapping is clearly a form of stealing.

Leviticus 19 expands our understanding even further. Yes, it is not just the hijacker, the burglar, the thief, kidnapper, or robber! Leviticus 19:11 begins with: "You shall not steal." Obviously that's the eighth commandment. Then it continues, "Nor deal falsely." Now to verse 13: "You shall not cheat your neighbor nor rob him."

God is trying to get the message through clearly: Don't steal, don't deal falsely, don't cheat, don't rob. If you're an employer of day laborers, notice the rest of verse 13: "The wages of him who is hired shall not remain with you all night until morning."

Traditionally day laborers were paid at the end of the day on which they worked.

Now look at Leviticus 19:15: "You shall do no injustice in judgment. You shall not be partial to the poor, nor honor the person of the mighty. But in righteousness you shall judge your neighbor." By the way, these are just a few passages. In many places the Bible talks about treating people properly– not robbing, not stealing. To capture the essence of these many references regarding stealing, let me share what some commentators have seen as examples of the violation of this law.

Dimensions of Dishonesty

Employers can be guilty of stealing when they demand longer work hours, or "downsize" the workforce to improve their profits. What about good salesmanship? Some people say, "Oh, I'm a good salesman," but actually what they are doing is called price gouging. And on the other hand, people say, "Oh, I drove a hard bargain," and sometimes the bargain hunter can be guilty of stealing.

Employees steal by taking office supplies, making long-distance phone calls, padding their expense reports, embezzling, or simply failing to put in a full day's work by idling away their time, through surfing the Internet, sending emails to friends, or playing computer games. Whenever we give anything less than our best effort, we are robbing our employer of the productivity we owe. In fact, employee theft costs the United States two hundred billion dollars a year.

Fraud, underpaying taxes, filling in false claims, theft of intellectual property, copyright violation including unlawful duplication of music and videos, are all forms of stealing. The government steals by wasting public money.

God forbids all greed and all abuse, including gambling. The Southern Baptist Convention puts it this way: "The Bible emphasizes the sovereignty of God in the direction of human events. Gambling looks to chance and good luck instead of to God. The Bible indicates that man is to work creatively and use his possessions for the good of others. Gambling fosters a good-for-nothing attitude." The Bible condemns covetousness and materialism. And, gambling has both at its heart. Gambling seeks personal gain and pleasure at another person's loss.

Any time that in anyway we try to gain an advantage for ourselves or even sometimes for others, we could be guilty of contravening this commandment.

And sometimes, we attempt to minimize our actions by using euphemistic terms. For example, in one country that threw off the yoke of oppression, people referred to stealing as "repossession." In another country, a TV journalist referred to "fuzzy math," when discussing deliberate fraud. Isn't it time to be more forthright and "call a spade a spade"?

The Real Reason for "Robbery"

The above examples show that stealing covers a broad sweep of activities. But, the question is: Why do people steal? Why do humans have this desire? What part does motive play?

One might give this answer from Jeremiah 17:9: "The heart is deceitful above all things, and desperately wicked." A fitting answer.

But, I believe we can identify at least three primary reasons for our wanting something that does not belong to us: we are not content, we covet, and we lack trust in God. This matter of coveting and contentment will be looked at later, as we study the meaning of the tenth commandment.

For now, let's consider the words of Jesus in Matthew 6:31-32: "Therefore, do not worry, saying, 'What shall we eat?' or 'What shall we drink?' or 'What shall we wear?' For after all these things the Gentiles seek. For your heavenly Father knows that you need all these things." And what does God do? He provides them. So the big question is, Do you, do I, trust God enough to say, "Lord, I know you will provide. I don't have to worry about these things."

Psalm 84:11 reiterates this point: "No good thing will He withhold from those who walk uprightly." Beautiful promise, isn't it? What does it say? God won't hold back anything good. If we trust in God, we will not have any desire to steal!

David says in Psalm 37:25: "I have been young, and now am old, yet I have not seen the righteous forsaken, nor his descendants begging bread." In simple terms, David knew that God would provide. Let's trust God to take care of us!

Science Supports Scripture

One of the reasons people steal is that they are not satisfied with what God has given them. Everyone wants happiness, wants fulfillment, wants meaning in life. All of us want to be happy. People think that the accumulation of things will provide that satisfaction that we all so naturally desire.

A psychologist at the University of California at Riverside, Sonja Lyubomirsky, has put together from her own study and the study of others eight steps to achieving fulfillment, all of which seem to harmonize positively with the Bible. Science has rediscovered what is already in the Bible. So I'm going to give you Bible texts which corroborate this scientific evidence.

Time magazine of January 17, 2005 states: "Money can't buy happiness. The things that really matter in life are not sold in stores. Love, friendship, family, respect, a place in the community, the belief that your life has purpose – those are the essentials of human fulfillment and they cannot be purchased with cash." Rather than cash, here are the keys to happiness.

Key #1: Count your blessings

Remember the words of that well-known song: "Count your many blessings; name them one by one." Deuteronomy 28:2-10 says several times that the Lord will bless us in many ways: in the city, in the country, with our produce, with our families – in so many ways. We can count the many blessings that God has given us. Psychologists suggest that we write a gratitude journal to actually keep track of the blessings.

In my own prayer life, Sabbath morning is the day that I take time for prayers of gratitude. Every Sabbath morning I review the week that has passed and say, "Thank you Lord for this. I'm grateful for that. I appreciate this and that." Sabbath mornings are exciting as I look back at the many blessings with which God has blessed me.

Key #2: Practice acts of kindness

This is a directive from the science of happiness. What does the Bible say? In Matthew 25:34-40 Jesus tells about people who were kind to the Lord without even realizing it – they fed the hungry, clothed the naked, entertained strangers, and visited those in prison. Jesus said, "Inasmuch as you did it to one of the least of these My brethren, you did it to Me." Scientists are correct when they say not to limit our kindness to our friends. They say practice random kindness – be kind to both friends and strangers.

Key #3: Savor life's joys

What does that mean? For one thing, don't rush your meals. When you sit down to eat a meal, select whatever it may be that you're going to eat, and take a few moments to let the juices flow and just enjoy the goodness of God.

Go outside. Walk in the sunshine. Watch as the sun is setting and appreciate the beauty provided by the Great Artist as He paints the evening sky. Psalm 19:1 states: "The heavens declare the glory of God; and the firmament shows His handiwork." Enjoy these beautiful things supplied by God.

Key # 4: Thank a mentor

In Ephesians 1:15-16, Paul writes: "I ... do not cease to give thanks for you."

Recently, a professor friend I had worked with at a university called and said, "Ron, I was thinking about you for such and such." After we had chatted a bit, I said, "You know what, I so appreciate the fact that you were a mentor to me." This religion professor had gotten a special award because of his excellent teaching. I began to watch him and to mimic him to learn from him. He became a mentor. And within five years, I was privileged to receive the same award because of his excellent example. I was happy to say, "Thank you for being such a great mentor in my life."

Key #5: Learn to forgive

In his book *The Art of Forgiving*, Lewis Smedes says, "Forgiveness is the key to the entire Christian agenda" (page 44). Smedes says that when we forgive, we walk in stride with the forgiving God.

We must learn to forgive. We pray, "Forgive us the wrong we have done, as we have forgiven those who have wronged us" (Matthew 6:12 NEB). And God replies, "If you forgive others the wrongs they have done, your heavenly Father will also forgive you; but if you do not forgive others, then your Father will not forgive the wrongs that you have done" (Matthew 6:14-15).

Strong's Concordance gives the following meanings for the word "forgive": "to send forth, to lay aside, to leave, to let go, to omit, to put away." So let's put away our slights, our anger, our grudges, our enmity and "be kind to one another, tenderhearted, forgiving one another, just as God in Christ also forgave you" (Ephesians 4:32). As hard as it may be, let's learn to forgive.

Key #6: Invest time/energy in family/friends

Proverbs 17:17 states, "A friend loves at all times." And of course we've already dealt with Exodus 20:12: "Honor your father and your mother that your days may be long."

Key #7: Take care of your body

If we want to be happy, if we want to have a fulfilling, meaningful life, we must take care of our bodies. We already touched on that before, so a brief reminder will do. "Do you not know that you are the temple of God and that the Spirit of God dwells in you? If anyone defiles the temple of God, God will destroy him. For the temple of God is holy, which temple you are" (1 Corinthians 3:16-17).

Key #8: Develop ways to cope with stress

Romans 8:35, 38-39 asks, "Who shall separate us from the love of Christ? Shall tribulation, or distress, or persecution, or famine, or nakedness, or peril, or sword?... I am persuaded that neither death nor life, nor angels nor principalities nor powers, nor things present nor things to come, nor height nor depth, nor any other created thing, shall be able to separate us from the love of God which is in Christ Jesus our Lord."

As I read that *Time* magazine article, and as I went back to the Scriptures, I concluded that in this area, these social scientists were right on target. Go ahead and put these eight scripturally-sound ideas into practice in your life, and you will enjoy a more meaningful and satisfying existence – your trust in God and His goodness will grow steadily!

How to Clear One's Conscience

Allow me to share a personal story, as I illustrate a vital issue regarding a "cure" for stealing. I was a single young man, toward the end of my teen years. I happened to be about a thousand miles from home, far away from my mother whom I loved dearly. I called home one day; and even though I had no money, I said, "Mom, I'm going to be home for Christmas."

Days went by, and I didn't know how to get home other than to hitch-hike. So I went and stood beside the road with my thumb out. I stood there and waited and waited and waited. A driver stopped, picked me up, and took me 300 miles to the next city. Oh, I was so happy. I was about one-third of the way home. But there I got stuck.

Day after day I would go out and stand all day long, but couldn't get a ride. Eventually desperation took over. Notice I didn't say I was focusing on God. What took over? Desperation. And it's a dangerous situation when desperation takes over.

So I went to the train station that day. I had no money. The train stopped, I jumped on board. I took a dive under the seat in a second-class compartment. Yes, I became a stowaway.

I lay under that seat for something like eighteen hours. It was such a small gap; and I still remember vividly that every time I turned my head, my nose would scrape on the floor. It was not comfortable there, in more than one way! The city where I jumped on the train was the hottest city in the country. Because of the heat and because of my fear of being discovered, I sweated my way down to Cape Town.

Yes, I got a "free ride." But the free ride was not really free. My conscience bothered me. The Holy Spirit began to impress me: "Ron, you have stolen from the railways." Ezekiel 33:15 says: If the thief "returns what he has stolen,... he will surely live."

Isn't a stowaway somebody who steals? Yes. But, as I said, I didn't have money. I began to work, and when I had money, I went to the railway office.

Admittedly, it had taken me about two years for my conscience to bring me fully to task. Having to make restitution to the railway was humiliating and a bit frightening. But, I needed to clear my conscience.

"Hello. Excuse me, sir. Ah, can you help me?"

"Yes, with what?"

"I would like to know what the price was of a second-class ticket – that is, a second class ticket two years ago."

"What are you asking?"

"I just need to know the price of a ticket two years ago."

"From where?"

"From Kimberley to Cape Town."

"Ah, okay, hold on. We'll check our records."

The agent went and checked their records, came back, and said, "Okay, this is the price of it. Why do you want to know?"

"Well, I have a confession to make. Back then, I stowed away on the train. And I have come today to pay my bill."

The man looked at me. "What?"

"Yes, I have come to pay for the ticket. I got the ride. I've just come to pay for my ticket."

The agent took the money, went away, and came back with the receipt.

I rushed home all excited. The burden was gone! What wonderful peace filled the place where the guilt had been. In fact, I was so nervous that I didn't even read what the agent had written on the receipt.

Later, when I looked at the receipt, I noticed two things written upon it: the cash amount and two words in big, bold letters: "**Conscience Money**."

Ah, conscience money. And, my conscience was clear at last.

When you or I have taken what doesn't belong to us, what do we have to do? We need to restore, repay (Ezekiel 33:15). Remember what Zacchaeus said in Luke 19:8: "If I have cheated anybody out of anything, I will pay back four times the amount."

That's what we are called upon to do, to give back if we have ever done wrong.

Positive Use of Possessions

Thus far, we have been looking at what some may call the "negative" side of the commandment "Thou shalt not steal." But, let's take some time to consider how we need to relate to the things we have been blessed with.

Psalm 24:1 says that God owns everything. He owns not only the cattle on a thousand hills but also the hills themselves. The earth is the Lord's. Every good thing belongs to the Lord. Every one of us is accountable to God for everything that He has placed under our care.

Remember the story that Jesus told of the "talents" given to the different people. And at the end, they brought what they had gained from investing the money. And the master said to each one who had been a faithful manager, "Well done, good and faithful servant" (Matthew 25:21, 23). That's right, stewardship means doing the right thing, the right way – using what God has blessed us with.

Stewardship relates to various factors, which can be briefly summarized as the four T's: temple (i.e., our body), time, treasures, and talents. Proper stewardship actually covers all these aspects. We will explore just the matter of "treasures" further.

In Malachi 3:10 God declares: "'Bring all the tithes into the storehouse, that there may be food in My house. And prove Me now in this,' says the Lord of hosts, 'if I will not open for you the windows of heaven and pour out for you such blessing that there will not be room enough to receive it.'" Now, it says tithes, and sometimes we just focus on that, but go back to verse 8 to get a broader context here. "'Will a man rob God? Yet, you have robbed Me! But you say, "In what way have we robbed You?" [And God responds:] 'In tithes and offerings. You are cursed with a curse, for you have robbed Me, even this whole nation.'"

A friend of mine put it this way: "The Bible itself indicates that withholding tithe was tantamount to robbing God Himself and would bring a curse. Well, I don't know about you, but I simply cannot conjure up a vision of some wretched miscreant so brazen, so cretinous, so brutish as to attempt to rob God."

"Financial" Security for the Future

The words of John Wesley, just twelve words. Write them down. Just a dozen simple words. John Wesley says that every Christian should do three things: "Earn all you can. Save all you can. Give all you can." This is what we are called upon as Christians to do.

One last scriptural passage, Matthew 6:19-21: "Do not lay up for yourselves treasures on earth, where moth and rust destroy and where thieves break in and steal; but lay up for yourselves treasures in heaven, where neither moth nor rust destroys and where thieves do not break in and steal. For where your treasure is, there your heart will be also."

"Do not" sounds almost like the "Thou shalt not..." of the eighth commandment. Do not lay up treasures here on earth, but do lay up treasures where? In heaven.

What does that mean? How do we do that?

Her name was Hetty Green. Her father was wealthy. When he died in 1864, he left Hetty a million U.S. dollars in cash and four million dollars in investments and properties. Hetty began to speculate: "Why did my father die? Ah, I wonder if somebody poisoned him."

And so Hetty began to live in fear and began to do all kinds of strange things. As she walked down the street, she would check to see if anybody was following her and dart into a little doorway and keep checking. And they say that when she went home at night, she slept under the bed. She left the bed made up, so that if anybody broke in they wouldn't think she was home.

Hetty Green did not buy new clothes, but wore the same dress day in and day out. She didn't buy any soap because it cost too much money. And so she wore the same dirty dress day in and day out.

Even worse, when her son broke his leg in a sledding accident, she refused to pay for medical treatment. The leg got infected. Surgeons had to amputate her son's leg.

At home, what did she eat? She ate cold oatmeal because it cost too much money to heat the food.

In 1916, while arguing vigorously with her maid over the price of milk, Hetty Green had a stroke and died – died like a pauper. Her father's investments had grown so that Hetty died owning more than one-hundred million dollars. With all that money Hetty Green was actually very, very "poor." She became known as the Witch of Wall Street.

Probably not many of us have one-hundred million dollars stashed away somewhere, but all of us have great treasures God has given us. We have life. We have time. We have talents. God has given us great treasures. And as His stewards, we have been offered the greatest treasure – that of eternal life. It's yours and mine for the asking! We can "possess" the greatest treasure of all, if we will accept God's gift of salvation by grace through faith in Jesus Christ (Ephesians 2:8-10).

Chapter 9
Small Spark – Big Bang!

"And God spoke all these words, saying:
'You shall not bear false witness
against your neighbor.'"
(Exodus 20:1, 16 NKJV)

According to a 1997 report, one-third of all adults in the United States of America believe that in our contemporary society lying is sometimes a necessity. The previous year, 91% of Americans surveyed confessed that they regularly don't tell the truth. What is happening to truth-telling? Can one trust what people say anymore?

The Trinity of Truth

Just hours before Jesus' crucifixion Pilate asked Him, "What is truth?" The irony of the question is that Pilate was looking at the Truth Himself, Jesus Christ, and he didn't even realize it!

Earlier on, Jesus had declared: "I am the way, the truth, and the life" (John 14:6). Jesus classified Himself as the Truth. A couple of chapters later, we find Jesus saying: "When He, the Spirit of truth, has come, He will guide you into all truth" (John 16:13). So Jesus calls the Holy Spirit the "Spirit of truth." God the Father is also recognized in Scripture as a God of Truth. Titus 1:2 says that God "cannot lie."

So with this background – that Jesus is the Truth, the Holy Spirit is the Truth, and God the

Father is the Truth – notice that, in the creation account in Genesis 1:27, "God created man in His own image." If we are made in His image, then we are supposed to reflect the triune God of Truth. And Matthew 5:16 says, "Let your light so shine before men, that they may see your good works and glorify your Father in heaven." We human beings, who serve a God of truth, are called upon to reflect that God, the God who is absolutely honest, totally trustworthy and transparent, the One in whom His created beings can have complete confidence.

Deceptions in Daily Life

The ninth commandment says "You shall not bear false witness against your neighbor." At times people say, "Oh, but I don't lie." But, sometimes we do lie to avoid embarrassment, don't we? "I'm really sorry, Mrs. Smith. We couldn't finish your job last night because the machine was broken." Yet the truth may be that you forgot all about the job. If you don't want to hurt somebody's feelings, you might say, "Thank you for sending those muffins – they were delicious!" But the truth might be that you took one bite and threw the rest away. To get a better grade, you say to your professor, "Sir, I finished the paper, but you know, just when I was about to print it, the electricity went off." That's the modern version of "My dog ate my homework!"

Let's look again at the ninth commandment: "You shall not bear false witness against your neighbor" (Exodus 20:16 NKJV). Put a little differently in the New International Version, this commandment reads: "You shall not give false testimony against your neighbor." That sounds like courtroom language, doesn't it? And so some have proclaimed, "This is legal language; it forbids perjury." Unfortunately, some have gone as far as to say that the prohibition on bearing false testimony is actually restricted to the courtroom. Thus, they assert that other kinds of lying are acceptable.

Legal Setting & the Law on Lying

It's true that the language of the ninth commandment does put it in a kind of legal setting, but let's look at how the Scripture itself interprets the ninth commandment. How do the Bible writers understand this commandment? You may remember that Leviticus 19 contains a reiteration of the Ten Commandments. Though the form may be different, basically all of the commandments are found in this chapter. For example, verse 3 says, "Everyone of you shall revere his mother and his father" – a reminder of the fifth commandment. The next line in that same verse, "and keep My Sabbaths," echoes the fourth commandment. In the next verse we read, "Do not turn to idols" – the second commandment. With a careful reading, you can find all 10 commandments in Leviticus 19, including the ninth, the one about "bearing false witness."

Let's look at verse 11 a little bit more carefully. "You shall not steal, nor deal falsely, nor lie to one another." Moses, the author of Leviticus as well as Exodus, was inspired to write this: "Nor lie to one another." The Hebrew word for "lie," *kachash*, is used broadly throughout the Old Testament, and it encompasses every kind of deception.

We can see this in the New Testament, too. In Colossians 3:9, Paul says, "Do not lie to one another." It sounds as though he's taking direct quotation from the Old Testament, doesn't it? But Paul doesn't just mention it; he goes on to explain why. Notice the next words: "Do not lie to one another, since you have put off the old man with his deeds and have put on the new man who is renewed in knowledge according to the image of Him who created him."

Paul explains why he is calling upon believers not to deceive anymore. In other words, he is saying, "You used to be spiritually dead. You were not a believer. But now you have put aside the old person, and you have become a new person, renewed in the knowledge according to the image of him who created him."

If we back up for a moment to Colossians 1, we can see Paul identifying Jesus, the Son of God, as the active agent in creation: "He [Jesus] is the image of the invisible God, the firstborn over all creation, For by Him all things were created that are in heaven and that are on earth" (Colossians 1:15, 16). So in chapter 3, when Paul talks about the believer who "is renewed in ... the image of Him who created him," he's obviously talking about Jesus, the active agent of creation.

Paul is saying "Folks, we understand why you used to lie when you were unbelievers. But now that you are Christians, you should not use deception, because you are becoming like Jesus Christ, the Truth."

Read how this idea is phrased in a book called *Thoughts from the Mount of Blessing* (page 68): "Everything that Christians do should be as transparent as the sunlight. Truth is of God; deception, in any one of its myriad forms, is of Satan; and whoever in any way departs from the straight line of truth is betraying himself into the power of the wicked one. Yet it is not a light or an easy thing to speak the exact truth. We cannot speak the truth unless we know the truth.... We cannot speak the truth unless our minds are continually guided by Him who is truth."

The only way you and I can speak the truth is if our minds are continually guided by Jesus Christ. It's only possible to be truly transparent, trustworthy people if we have our minds filled with Jesus Christ, the Way, the Truth, and the Life. We are to follow the example of Christ, the One in whom "no deceit was found in his mouth" (1 Peter 2:21, 22).

Deception = Disaster and Death

This commitment to truth-telling is a very important matter, because it has eternal results. John found it important enough to bring it up three times in the last two chapters of Revelation. The first time, he's talking about the end of time: "He who overcomes shall inherit all things, and I will be his God and he shall be My son. But the cowardly, unbelieving, abominable, murderers, sexually immoral, sorcerers, idolaters, and *all liars* shall have their part in the lake which burns with fire and brimstone, which is the second death" (Revelation 21:7, 8). This issue of lying is serious business!

The second occurrence is in verse 27. Referring to the restored New Jerusalem, it says: "But there shall by no means enter [the city] anything that defiles, or causes an abomination or a *lie*." Finally, again talking about those who will be in the New Jerusalem, John notes, "Blessed are those who do His commandments, that they may have the right to the tree of life, and may enter through the gates into the city. But outside are...sexually immoral and murders and idolaters, and *whoever loves and practices a lie*" (Revelation 22:15).

Subtle Forms of Subterfuge

The issue of truth-telling is a vital issue, with eternal implications. That is why we need to spend some time looking at it. Back in the Old Testament, Proverbs 12:22 says, "Lying lips are an *abomination* unto the Lord." Strong word! When I was young, my parents made sure I memorized this passage. Unfortunately, in a kind of unintentional pharisaical manner, I limited this counsel to only lying *lips*.

I'll admit, I wasn't a very honest kid at heart. I remember once when the dormitory dean came into my room and asked, "Ron, do you know who did such and such?" Because I knew I shouldn't lie with my lips, I shrugged my shoulders and asked, "How must I know, sir?" I didn't say, "I don't know." I attempted to salve my conscience by telling myself that I didn't lie with my lips, even though my very actions had communicated the lie non-verbally.

What does the Bible say about this? "A scoundrel and a villain, who goes about with a corrupt mouth, who winks with his eye, signals with his feet and motions with his fingers, who plots evil with deceit in his heart – he always stirs up dissension" (Proverbs 6:12 NIV). A non-verbal lie is still a lie, isn't it? Consider how this is put in the book *Patriarchs and Prophets* (page 309): "False speaking in any matter, every attempt or purpose to deceive our neighbor, is here included. An intention to deceive is what constitutes falsehood. By a glance of the eye, a motion of the hand, an expression of the countenance, a falsehood may be told as effectually as by words. All intentional overstatement, every hint or insinuation…, even the statement of facts in such a manner so as to mislead, is falsehood."

Further Forms of Falsehood

Let's continue to explore what the Bible says. "You shall not circulate a false report" (Exodus 23:1 NKJV). In other words, don't spread rumors. In Leviticus 19, the chapter that expands and clarifies principles of the Ten Commandments, we read, "Do not go about spreading slander among your people" (verse 16). So the command about bearing false witness is not just for the courtroom. It's also about slander or gossip.

Notice what the wise man, Solomon, says: "A wicked man listens to evil lips; a liar pays attention to a malicious tongue" (Proverbs 17:4 NIV). Have you ever said, "Oh, but I'm not the one sharing the gossip, I just happen to hear it"? But Solomon is saying that you are guilty of gossip even if you dare to listen to it! Paul counsels the Corinthians to keep away from slander, gossip, and evil reports (2 Corinthians 12:20).

The tongue is a powerful thing! James 3:3 points out how the bit in the horse's mouth can be used to make the animal obey. In verse 4, he notes how a ship's rudder can turn the whole ship. "Even so the tongue is a little member, and boasts great things. See how great a forest a little fire kindles" (verse 5). A small spark can cause a big bang!

Let's read further: "And the tongue is a fire, a world of iniquity. The tongue is so set among our members that it defiles the whole body, and sets on fire the course of nature; and it is set on fire by hell…. But no man can tame the tongue. It is an unruly evil, full of deadly poison. With it we bless our God and Father, and with it we curse men, who have been made in the similitude of God. Out of the same mouth proceed blessing and cursing" (verses

6-10). And then James makes this appeal: "My brethren, these things ought not to be so" (verse 10). Powerful words – about the power of words!

Reflect Before You Respond

So what does Jesus admonish us to do? In His Sermon on the Mount, Jesus cautions His hearers to be careful that they don't swear by heaven, by the earth, or by their heads (Matthew 5:34-36). "Simply let your 'Yes' be 'Yes,' and your 'No,' 'No'; anything beyond this comes from the evil one" (verse 37). This is vital counsel from Jesus Himself.

I had the privilege some years ago to work for a genuine Christian gentleman. His life was a fine example of Paul's words in 1 Corinthians 11:1: "Imitate me, just as I also imitate Christ." As I worked for this man for a few years, I noticed that every time we talked, before he would respond to a question, he would pause for a moment. Then he would look at me and carefully, clearly, compassionately, and in a Christ-centered way, he would answer my question. I was amazed. I remember thinking, "I want to be like him," because he was reflecting Jesus Christ constantly. This man spoke in such a way that the tongue was not a "small spark – big bang." Instead, he was always uplifting Jesus Christ through his speech patterns.

Why is it so important to be like Jesus in how we speak? Jesus Himself answers our question. Speaking to a group of hypocrites: "Brood of vipers! How can you, being evil, speak good things? For out of the abundance of the heart the mouth speaks. A good man out of the good treasure of his heart brings forth good things, and an evil man out of the evil treasure brings forth evil things. But I say to you that for every idle word men may speak, they

will give account of it in the day of judgment"
(Matthew 12:34-36 NKJV).

Pause a moment and think about your own life.
In the judgment, you must give account for every
idle word you have spoken. Now look at the next
verse: "For by your words you will be justified, and
by your words you will be condemned" (verse 37).
Do you understand the importance of this message?
This is a serious issue, very vital for salvation. By
your words you will be justified, by your words you
will be condemned. Think about what you say.
Make sure that your heart is with the Lord.

Communicate Compassionately

We already read Proverbs 12:22: "Lying lips are
an abomination to the Lord." And since, as Jesus
says, "out of the abundance of the heart the mouth
speaks," we know that lies spring forth from a
deceptive heart. Proverbs 12:20 confirms this:
"Deceit is in the heart of those who devise evil." In
contrast, verse 17 describes the one whose heart
isn't full of deceit: "He who speaks truth declares
righteousness."

So we are challenged to speak the truth. This is
corroborated in Ephesians 4:29: "Do not let any
unwholesome talk come out of your mouths, but
only what is helpful for building others up according
to their needs" (NIV). There is the challenge for us.
When we speak, are our words always helpful for
building up one another?

And verse 15 tells us that we should be
"speaking the truth in love." Sometimes a person
says, "I told her the truth and she needs to hear it."
That isn't speaking the truth in love. I like how the
New Century Version translates Psalm 141:3. It

reads like a prayer, one that I believe each one of us must pray. "Lord, help me control my tongue. Help me be careful about what I say." If we pray this prayer, we're more apt to speak the truth in love.

The Lord, and Lying to Save Life

Earlier I quoted from a book which rightly noted that "deception in every one of its myriad forms is of Satan." But what about a case of lying to save life? Sometime ago I read an article titled "In Defense of Rahab," written by a friend of mine. In his article, he said in essence: "Rahab lied to save life; she did the right thing; we should follow Rahab." And I said, "God forbid that we should follow a practicing prostitute." She should not be our model for morality. Scripture is crystal clear that Jesus Christ alone is our example for ethics.

Once a woman came to me after I had given a lecture and asked me, "But pastor, what should we do about lying in those issues of life or death?"

I asked her, "Sister, if Jesus were there in Rahab's situation, would He have lied? Would Jesus have used deception?"

Now I know with certainty that He would not have lied. The Bible tells us repeatedly that Jesus never committed any sin. As 1 Peter 2:21 (NIV) records, "To this you were called, because Christ suffered for you, leaving you an example, that you should follow in his steps." Not in Rahab's steps. Not even in Abraham's steps. Only in Jesus' steps. And verse 22 says "He [Jesus] committed no sin, and no deceit was found in his mouth."

The only sin that is specifically mentioned in this verse is the one we all seem to go for so easily, those so-called "little white lies"! The Greek word used here for "deceit" is *dolos*, a word that covers every form of deception. We must imitate the truthfulness of Jesus! He is our model for morality.

Which is why I asked that lady, "Would Jesus have used deception?"

And she said, "No."

"What would he have done?" I queried.

She looked at me and said, "He could have been silent." Yes, just as He remained silent in front of Pilate and Herod. Or He could have prayed and asked God to intervene. There were various options. And so this woman and I agreed that, as the Bible indicates, Jesus would never have used deception.

Fearless of the Future, and Faithful

Let me share with you some biblical counsel on this issue. Revelation 2 and 3 are calls to the early Christian churches to be faithful, to be fearless, to stand firm in the face of trials. In chapter 2, verse 10, we read, "Do not fear any of those things which you are about to suffer." In simple terms, John is admonishing them – and us – to live fearless of the future. And at the end of this verse is a call: "Be faithful unto death, and I [i.e., Jesus] will give you the crown of life." Be faithful unto death!

In Revelation 12:11 we read a word picture of those who are faithful unto death: "And they overcame him [the devil] by the blood of the Lamb and by the word of their testimony. And they did not love their lives to the death." In simple terms, they were faithful.

Leave Consequences with the Creator

Ecclesiastes 8:7 (NET) declares, "Surely, no one knows the future." So if no one knows the future, why are we thinking, "I had better lie because this is going to happen"? There's no point in lying to change a future outcome.

We can't predict what will happen five minutes from now, much less the future! We shouldn't worry about the future. In fact, Solomon, the wise man, puts it this way: "Foolish people claim to know all about the future" (Ecclesiastes 10:14 NET).

In short, "True Christian principles will not stop to weigh consequences" (*Sanctified Life*, page 39). Put simply, "We should choose the right because it is right and leave consequences with God" (*The Great Controversy*, page 460).

How did Jesus relate to this issue of results? In His Sermon on the Mount, Jesus addressed people who don't have enough faith: "O you of little faith? Therefore do not worry, saying 'What shall we eat?' or 'What shall we drink?' or 'What shall we wear?' For after all these things the Gentiles [or 'the unconverted' NET] seek. For your Heavenly Father knows that you need all these things. But seek first the kingdom of God and His righteousness, and all these things shall be added to you" (Matthew 6:30-33). In other words, Jesus is saying, "Don't worry about the future; leave all results in God's hands; trust Him!"

The reality is that, "Our only safe course is to render obedience to all His commandments at whatever cost" (*Testimonies for the Church*, Volume 5, page 365). That's the challenge. In the same book, in accord with Revelation 2:10, it states, "Death before dishonor or the transgression of God's law should be the motto of every Christian" (page 147). Is that our motto? "It is better to die than to sin; better to want than to defraud; better to hunger than to lie" (*Testimonies for the Church,*

Volume 4, page 495). It couldn't have been said more clearly.

Faithfulness to God's call for truthfulness does not guarantee that all will go well. There might be challenges. Notice this statement: "The season of distress before God's people will call for a faith that will not falter. His children will make it manifest that He is the only object of their worship and that no consideration, not even of life itself, can induce them to make the least confession to false worship. To the loyal heart the commands of sinful, finite men will sink into insignificance beside the word of the Eternal God. Truth will be obeyed though the result be imprisonment or exile or death" (*Prophets and Kings*, pages 512-513). That is God's call to us. Remember John the Baptizer? His truthful challenge to King Herod of his immoral life, cost him his life.

Martyred for the Master

The story is told of Dr. Boris Kornfeld, a political prisoner in the Gulag in former Communist Russia. Because he was a physician, Dr. Kornfeld was required by his captors to sign death certificates for people who died in the prison. For those who died as a result of torture, brutal beatings, and starvation, he was forced to sign certificates to send to Moscow stating that the prisoner had died "from natural causes."

In time, Dr. Kornfeld met a true believer in Jesus, in the prison. Through the influence of this Christian, he too became a Christian.

As Kornfeld began to understand what it meant to live as a true Christian, to have Jesus Christ in his life, to follow the Way, the Truth, and the Life, he realized that he needed to stop signing those false reports. He couldn't continue to practice deception now that he was committed to the Truth!

Boris Kornfeld knew that this was no small decision. His captors would not be pleased. But he decided that he was going to be faithful unto death!

So, he went to a fellow political prisoner, and said, "Sasha, you know that I've become a Christian. I'm going to follow my Lord, to follow Jesus, even if I will die. So I've started signing these certificates 'death from torture,' 'death from brutal beatings,' 'death from starvation,' and am sending them to Moscow. When Moscow contacts the wardens, I know what will very likely happen. So, if you hear a commotion at night, please check to see if I'm okay."

It wasn't long before the reports came back from Moscow to the wardens, "Why are you beating, torturing, and starving people to death in the prison?" Soon thereafter, one fateful night, Sasha heard a commotion. After the guards had left, he went and checked on his friend, Boris Kornfeld. Sure enough, tragically, Kornfeld had been brutally beaten to death. Dr. Kornfeld had died faithful to Jesus Christ.

The event didn't pass by unnoticed. Sasha was so touched by what it means to live and die for the Lord that he gave his life to Jesus, too. Sasha, by the way, is the Russian nickname for Alexander. And that's how Alexander Solzhenitsyn, the great writer, became a Christian. The old saying rings with truth: "The blood of the martyrs is the seed of the church."

This "forgotten" martyr, Dr. Boris Kornfeld, is a testimony to a life lived with Jesus in the heart.

Turn to Jesus, the Truth

The only way we can be totally truthful, transparent people is if we have Jesus Christ living in our hearts. That's the call to us today.

In order to keep the ninth commandment, we don't need to worry about trying to not tell lies. Instead, we need to focus on spending time with the written Word, so we can have the Living Word, Jesus Christ, in our lives. Then what we say and what we do, the way we live our lives, will reveal a transparent picture of Jesus Christ, the Way, the Truth, and the Life.

When we stand tall as truthful Christians amidst a forest of lies, people around us will trust us, and more importantly, they will see Jesus Christ and be attracted to Him. In brief, this *guideline for a great life* is a direct appeal to live as people of integrity!

Chapter 10
Secrets for Stressless Living

"And God spoke all these words, saying:
'You shall not covet your neighbor's
house; you shall not covet your
neighbor's wife; nor his male servant,
nor his female servant, nor his ox,
nor his donkey, nor anything
that is your neighbor's.'"
(Exodus 20:1, 17 NKJV)

Mrs. Sharpe was taking her dog, Jonathan, for a walk near her home in Los Angeles. Responsible dog owner that she was, she always took a utensil and a plastic bag with her so she could pick up anything that Jonathan left behind when he did his business. This evening was no exception. Jonathan had finished his business and they were on their way home when Mrs. Sharpe started having an uneasy sense that something wasn't right. She glanced over her shoulder and saw nothing. "Oh, it must be my imagination," she thought as she kept walking. But she continued to feel that something was wrong. Looking over her shoulder again, she saw him – a man lurking in the shadows. Mrs. Sharpe hurried on towards the safety of her home, but before she could get there, the man dashed out, grabbed her bag, and ran away – carrying a plastic bag full of Jonathan's business! Too many times, that's the way it is in life.

We desire what others have and we end up holding the bag.

Coveting Is Commendable!

We've been on a journey together through the Ten Commandments – the guidelines for a great life– digging into God's Word; and we've discovered many blessings. Now we're on the last leg of that journey.

Coveting is good. Yes, you read that right – coveting is good! That sounds contradictory, doesn't it? Especially since we're about to look at the tenth commandment, which some have thought says, "Thou shalt not covet." Actually, it doesn't say that. Before you call me a heretic and throw this book away, let me explain myself.

In 1 Corinthians 12:31, which is the introduction to chapter 13, we read: "But *covet* earnestly the best gifts: and yet I show unto you a more excellent way" (KJV). So the Bible actually calls upon us to *covet*. Though we often say "Don't covet," coveting in and of itself is not necessarily bad. The Hebrew term itself is actually neutral.

Back to the Beginning of Time

To explain this further, let's go back to the beginning, right after God created Adam. Genesis 2:9 reads: "And out of the ground the LORD God made every tree grow that is pleasant to the sight and good for food. The tree of life was also in the midst of the garden, and the tree of the knowledge of good and evil." The Hebrew word *chamad*, which is translated as "pleasant to the sight" here, also means "desirable," or "that which should be *coveted*." God made these things to be *coveted*, to be desired. God actually wants us to desire that which is good.

The problem comes in the next chapter, in Genesis 3:6, where the tree of the knowledge of good and evil, the forbidden tree, is spoken about. "So when the woman saw that the tree was good for food, that it was pleasant to the eyes, and a tree *desirable* to make one wise, she took of its fruit and ate." There's the same word *chamad* – the tree was *desirable*. So there is nothing wrong with coveting, with desiring something, unless you are coveting or desiring something which you should not desire. Eve was desiring the fruit of the tree which God had forbidden. There's the problem – desiring that which is not ours.

The "Dream" Turns into a Disaster

A problem that we all face nowadays is a desire to "keep up with the Joneses." Here in the United States we often refer to this as the "American Dream" – ambition, work hard, get all you can and keep all you can. Unfortunately, the American Dream has turned into the North American Nightmare for some people.

Modern media and its advertising campaigns create in us a desire for things. And so that's the problem. We are so inundated with this desire for things that more and more people are spending more and more money that they don't have. In the year 2005, more than two million people in the United States filed for personal bankruptcy. Why? Because people are spending to satisfy themselves with what they cannot afford. That's part of this whole problem of coveting. Our natural selfish hearts tend to go that way.

Two children, Kevin, age 5, and his 3-year-old brother Ryan, were waiting hungrily while their mother started preparing pancakes for them to eat for breakfast. Soon the boys started arguing over who would get the first pancake. Seeing the opportunity for a moral lesson, their mother said, "If Jesus were sitting here, He would say, 'Let my brother have the first pancake; I can wait.'" At this, Kevin turned to his younger brother and said, "Ryan, you be Jesus!"

Like these little children, our scheming hearts compel us to say to someone else, "you be Jesus," so they will be obliged to say, "Let my brother be first." Our naturally selfish hearts always want to be first. No wonder the tenth commandment is an important one.

Crucial Culminating Commandment

Let's look at the commandment itself now, in Exodus 20:17. I've already told you that the Hebrew word for coveting is actually neutral. This explains why the commandment has to be more than simply, "Thou shalt not covet." It's a long commandment, covering every possibility in dealing with the important things: "You shall not covet your neighbor's house; you shall not covet your neighbor's wife, nor his male servant, nor his female servant, nor his ox, nor his donkey, nor anything that is your neighbor's."

That last phrase in particular leaves no loopholes, does it? This command concerning coveting – desiring what isn't yours – includes everything. This really covers everything that you shouldn't covet, because it all belongs to someone else. Coveting is a good thing, if it's used to desire the best gifts. But coveting is a bad thing when you desire what doesn't belong to you.

A friend of mine once said, "People who obey the tenth commandment will be better prepared to obey the first nine." This is because it all starts in the heart, dealing with attitudes and motives. Then, my friend finished off his statement by saying that "people who break the tenth are on their way to breaking any of the rest of them." So the tenth commandment is very, very important.

One Bible commentator has described the impact of this tenth commandment on the other nine quite effectively. "Before Ahab's obsessive desire for Naboth's vineyard was satisfied, the ninth and sixth commandments had been broken. Before David's lust for Bathsheba was sated, the seventh, the eighth, and the sixth commandments were broken. The coveting merchants of Amos's day broke the fourth commandment and the eighth commandment in their fever to possess (see Amos 8). The citizens of Judah in Jeremiah's time, deifying their desires, longing for a material and local security, violated the first, the third, the sixth, the seventh, and the ninth commandments, and above all by making Yahweh's temple into a fetish, the second commandment as well. And the son whose determined desire for his own way led him to strike or abuse his father and mother was guilty of breaking the fifth commandment."

What has just been illustrated in simply one paragraph is that, when one violates the tenth commandment, every one of the previous nine commandments can be broken to satisfy the desires of the heart, to have that which doesn't belong to us.

The Spring of All Sin

The book *Sons and Daughters of God* (page 65) puts it this way: "The tenth commandment strikes at the very root of all sins, prohibiting the selfish desire, from which springs the sinful act." So this is a crucial commandment.

This commandment talks about the heart of the matter here. While people cannot read our hearts, we know that God can. "The Lord does not see as man sees; for man looks at the outward appearance, but the LORD looks at the heart" (1 Samuel 16:7). This tenth commandment is the only commandment that doesn't deal with action at all; rather, it deals with the heart, from which spring our attitudes, thoughts, motives, and actions.

This last commandment has implications for all the other nine that come before it. And so this commandment is pivotal; it's crucial. In fact, the great Protestant Reformer, Martin Luther, said that this commandment, the tenth commandment, more than any other shows us that we are sinners. And beyond that, it shows us our need of a Savior, Jesus Christ.

In Matthew 15:19, Jesus put it this way: "For out of the heart proceed evil thoughts, murders, adulteries, fornications, thefts, false witness, blasphemies." In contrast to these things, Jesus gives the following advice in Matthew 6:19: "Do not lay up for yourselves treasures on earth, where moth and rust destroy and where thieves break in and steal; but lay up for yourselves treasures in heaven, where neither moth nor rust destroys and where thieves do not break in and steal. For where your treasure is, there your heart will be also." Everything – good or evil – starts in the heart.

Remember what Jesus said about adultery in Matthew 5? "You have heard that it was said to those of old, 'You shall not commit adultery.'" But notice that Jesus doesn't limit this command to the act itself. He says, "Whoever looks at a woman to lust for her has already committed adultery with her in his heart" (verses 27, 28).

And so as we reflect on this whole issue of coveting, we have to ask, "Where is my heart? Where are my desires? Where do I want to place the importance of my heart?"

Coveting Can Be a Counterfeit God

Really, this all comes down to trusting in God. If you want something that you don't have, something that the Lord hasn't blessed you with, you are basically saying, "I don't trust you, God; You have not provided what I want." That's the key issue when it comes down to wanting what doesn't belong to you.

Paul amplifies Jesus' words about coveting, using uncomfortably strong language. "For this you know, that no fornicator, unclean person, nor covetous man, who is an idolater, has any inheritance in the kingdom of Christ and God" (Ephesians 5:5). In other words, the person who covets, even though no one knows about it, is as much a sinner as one who starts worshiping idols! As Paul noted, a covetous person is an idolater. This is a serious allegation! But it is biblical truth. It's a matter of priorities: either you put God first, or you let the things you covet come between you and God, becoming your gods, as it were. And so you become an idolater.

Notice Jesus' warning: "Take heed and beware of covetousness, for one's life does not consist in the abundance of the things he possesses" (Luke 12:15). Beware of covetousness!

A Cure for Covetousness?

But there is good news. The Bible gives us the remedy that heals the covetous heart, the idolater's heart. Isaiah 55:7 makes this summons: "Let the wicked forsake his way, And the unrighteous man his thoughts." We are called upon to forsake our evil thoughts, and that includes any covetous thoughts. We can make an actual choice to forsake, to give up these thoughts, to give up our sinful desires.

But we have to consciously make that choice. Because our thoughts and desires have often been shaped by the media that constantly surrounds us, we have to make a choice to have our thoughts reshaped. This can be an uphill battle, going against our natural and cultivated tendencies. Because it's easier to go downhill than to climb back up, wherever possible, we need to take care that we don't start down the hill. We have to make daily choices to forsake our covetous thoughts. These can be simple choices – not looking at certain magazines, turning off the television, walking away from unhealthy situations. We must forsake our covetous thoughts.

Remember David's infamous fall into sin, as recorded in 2 Samuel 11? He was carried away by his covetous thoughts and ended up breaking several other commandments. But when he eventually came to repentance, he prayed, "Create in me a clean heart, O God, and renew a right spirit within me" (Psalm 51:10). So, not only did he choose to forsake the sin, he also asked God to create in him a clean heart. Both aspects are desperately needed for covetous hearts.

Now notice God's promise: "I will put My law in their minds, and write it on their hearts; and I will be their God, and they shall be My people" (Jeremiah 31:33). This is a major part of the long-term solution to covetous hearts! First, we must forsake our unrighteous thoughts and ask God to create in us a clean heart. Then, God promises to put His law in our minds and write it on our hearts.

Contentment Through Christ

When that happens, our desires fall in line with God's will for us, and then we become more and more like the way Paul put it in Philippians 4:11: "For I have learned in whatever state I am, to be content."

Are we content, or not? We need to go to the feet of Jesus Christ and learn from Him how to be content. Paul addresses this in Philippians 2: "Let this mind be in you which was also in Christ Jesus" (verse 5); "and being found in appearance as a man, He humbled Himself and became obedient to the point of death, even the death of the cross" (verse 8). In other words, Jesus was one who was contented, humble, willing to do exactly what His Father called upon Him to do. That's the whole issue.

How does the Bible recommend that we meet this challenge? A single verse in Hebrews 13 gives us the solution to the covetous desires of our sinful hearts. Inspired by God, Paul writes, "Let your conduct be without covetousness; be content with such things as you have. For He Himself [i.e., Jesus] has said, 'I will never leave you nor forsake you'" (Hebrews 13:5). Notice the change of focus – rather than looking at material things, we should look to the Master, Jesus Christ. We should be satisfied with what we have because Jesus has said, "I will be with you." Rather than worrying if we have enough stuff, we should be asking if we have the Savior in our lives.

The solution to covetousness is learning to trust God. It's learning to say, "Lord, whatever You have provided is sufficient for me. I have learned under all circumstances to be content." The only way to do this is to have the mind of Christ in us. We can accomplish this by spending time in His Word, filling our minds with the Scriptures daily. The more we read, the more we understand, the more we accept, and the more we fill our minds with the mind of Christ through the written Word, the more contented we will become. Then we will not have a problem with coveting that which belongs to others.

Breaking a Habit with a Bracelet

Recently, I heard about a pastor who was tired of hearing people complain – they were just not content with life. He came up with a plan. He got a bunch of purple bracelets – enough for all of his church members. As he distributed them, he said, "I'm going to have you all wear this purple bracelet on your right wrist for 21 days. It's the 'No Complaining' bracelet. You can't complain while you're wearing this. You can't complain about the weather. You can't even complain about other people's complaining! If you catch yourself complaining, the moment you complain, you've got to move the bracelet to your left wrist. Then you have to start counting days all over again. If you complain again, it goes back to your right wrist and you start again at Day One. Keep this up until you have gone through 21 days with the purple bracelet staying on one wrist because you haven't uttered a single complaint."

The pastor admitted that this was difficult even for himself. His own bracelet kept moving back and forth, right to left and left to right as he caught himself complaining. But eventually, the purple bracelet stayed on one wrist for 21 days. This idea caught on. Soon people began asking that church to send them "No Complaining" bracelets. These little purple bracelets have been sent out freely by this church to more than 1.3 million people in over 80 different countries!

Psychologists have pretty much determined it takes three weeks – 21 days – to form a new habit. So if you can keep the "No Complaining" bracelet on the same wrist for 21 days, you won't complain anymore. What's this got to do with the tenth commandment? We need to quit complaining, to stop wishing we had what we don't, to stop coveting, and be content with what we have!

It Is God, Not the Goods

Paul counsels us with just this thought in Philippians 4:11-12 (NIV): "I am not saying this because I am in need, for I have learned to be content whatever the circumstances. I know what it is to be in need, and I know what it is to have plenty. I have learned the secret of being content in any and every situation, whether well fed or hungry, whether living in plenty or in want." Notice – *content* in *all* circumstances! Then Paul tells us the key to his success at being always contented: "I can do all things through Christ who strengthens me." Here it is again – "don't worry about things; make sure your focus is upon Jesus Christ."

Psalm 73 is a good example of learning to be content by focusing on the right place. In brief, Asaph, the writer of this psalm, says to God, "I looked around at the wicked and I noticed they were prospering. Lord, how can You allow this? This isn't fair!" Apparently, the problem within his heart was discontentment, perhaps even covetousness. But eventually he says, "I went into the sanctuary, and I met God there, and then I understood the end of the wicked." I love the conclusion Asaph comes to in verse 25: "Whom have I in heaven but You? And there is none upon earth that I desire besides You." Finally he gets his focus in the right place, on God, not on goods!

In Matthew 6:33, Jesus identifies this very secret to living a stressless life: "Seek first the kingdom of God and His righteousness, and all these things shall be added to you." If we focus upon God and His kingdom, if we recognize that He is everything rather than looking at things, He will satisfy us with all we need, and we will be content. Put simply: "For where your treasure is, there will your heart be also" (Matthew 6:21).

Jesus Is the Joy of Living

This tenth commandment is so important. It has many implications for our lives. Are we satisfied? Are we contented with Jesus Christ, or are we hankering after the things that others have?

Nelson Rockefeller was once asked, "How much money do you need to be satisfied?" And that billionaire said, "Just a little more." Too often, we want just a little more, something "better" – whether it be finances, a physical body, or even spiritual gifts that others are blessed with. So many times we are out searching for something that isn't ours, that belongs to someone else. We want what others have.

But when we focus on Jesus and are content with Him, when we seek first the kingdom of God and His righteousness, God promises, "I will take care of everything." Then we will be truly content. Follow this *guideline*, and you will have *a great life*!

Epilogue to the Decalogue
The End – Time for a Great Life

The story is told of a woman who pulls up to a red light behind one other car. She notices the driver of the car in front of her is talking on his cell phone and appears to be shuffling through some papers on the seat beside him. The light turns green, but the man doesn't notice. The woman waits, but the man still doesn't notice that the light has turned green. Frustrated, the woman begins pounding on her steering wheel and yelling at the man, but he still doesn't move. By this time, the light is turning yellow; she goes ballistic, blowing her horn and screaming curses at the man. Hearing the commotion, the man looks up, sees the yellow light, and accelerates through the intersection just as the light turns red. The woman is beside herself, screaming in frustration as she misses her chance to get through the intersection.

As she is still in mid-rant, she hears a tap on her window. She turns her head and finds herself looking up into the barrel of a gun held by a very serious looking policeman. The policeman tells her to shut off her car, while keeping both hands in sight. Dumbfounded, she complies with the order. After she shuts off the engine, the policeman orders her to exit her car with her hands up. She gets out of the car and he orders her to turn and place her hands on her car. She complies, and he immediately handcuffs her and hustles her into his patrol car. She is too bewildered by the rapid chain of events to ask any questions. She is driven to the police station, where she is fingerprinted, photographed, searched, booked, and placed in a cell.

After a couple of hours, another policeman approaches the cell door and opens it, beckoning for her to come out. She is escorted back to the booking desk, where the original officer is waiting with her personal effects. He hands her the bag containing her things and says, "I'm really sorry for this mistake. But you see, I pulled up behind your car while you were blowing your horn and cussing a blue streak at the car in front of you. And then I noticed the 'Choose Life' license plate holder, and the 'Follow me to Sunday School' bumper sticker, and the chrome-plated Christian fish emblem on the trunk, so naturally I assumed you had *stolen* the car."

We may smile at this woman's unfortunate experience – but our laughter is somewhat nervous, because to some degree the story is about us. Isn't that so?

The Law of Liberty

James talks about such a situation in his letter to the Christians of his day: "Out of the same mouth proceed blessing and cursing. My brethren, these things ought not to be so. Does a spring send forth fresh water and bitter from the same opening? Can a fig tree, my brethren, bear olives, or a grapevine bear figs? Thus no spring can yield both salt water and fresh" (James 3:10-12 NKJV).

If we look back at verse 6, we can clearly see that James is talking about the tongue: "And the tongue is a fire, a world of iniquity. The tongue is so set among our members that it defiles the whole body, and sets on fire the course of nature; and it is set on fire by hell." These are strong words!

Notice how this ties in with what he says in James 2:12: "So speak and so do as those who will be judged by the law of liberty." That's an interesting phrase, isn't it? "The law of liberty." He says that we're all going to be judged, according to what we say and what we do, by the law of liberty.

Which law is he talking about? If we back up two verses to get the context, we read that "whoever shall keep the whole law, and yet stumble in one point, he is guilty of all. For He who said, 'Do not commit adultery,' also said, 'Do not murder.'" Based on this context, we can see that the law James is talking about is the Ten Commandments – what he calls the "law of liberty."

Love the Lord = Live His Law

According to the Bible, loving our Lord is closely connected with living His law, this law of liberty. Consider these well-known words of Jesus, recorded in John 14:15 (NKJV): "If you love me, keep my commandments." Some newer translations, such as the New International Version, say: "If you love me, you *will* obey what I command." It's basically an automatic response of our love to obey Him.

1 John 5:3 expresses a similar idea: "For this is the love of God, that we keep His commandments. And His commandments are not burdensome." The New Century Version puts it another way: "And His commandments are not too hard to keep." According to the New Living Translation, "Loving God means keeping His commandments, and really, that isn't difficult."

Let's go to one more witness in the New Testament. Paul also mentions the issue of keeping the law. In Romans 13:10, he says, "Love does no harm to a neighbor; therefore love is the fulfillment of the law." If we understand correctly that "love is the fulfilling of the law," then there is no way that we can be accused of legalism. As long as love comes first! One Bible commentary says that "love is the motive power of obedience." Love for the Lord is what motivates us to live loyally according to His law of liberty.

Growing into These Godly Guidelines

Do you want to grow deeply in love with the Lord? Do you want to be able to automatically do what God in His law of liberty calls you to do? Wouldn't it be wonderful if we would always choose to instinctively do God's will, from virtually an automatic response?

In Luke 17:5, after Jesus has just talked about forgiving over and over again, the shocked disciples pleaded with the Lord: "Increase our faith." This is an important principle.

How can this happen? We need to pray more, to daily commune with God through the reading of the Bible, to put into practice what we learn, and to share His love with others. Remember, your faith will strengthen through continual exercise.

May these *Top Ten* principles, so graciously given by a loving God, be the *Guidelines for a Great Life* that you will enjoy both now and in the hereafter!